FIREFIGHT!

FIREFIGHT!
The History of Personal Firepower

Peter Newark

A David & Charles Military Book

ACKNOWLEDGEMENTS

I wish to express particular thanks to the following people, museums, institutions and other establishments for providing me with information and illustrations:

Patrick Robert Cobbe of Military Matters, Bath; Nicholas Wilkey; David Williams of Christie's South Kensington; Alex de Chair of Sotheby's; Department of the Navy, US Marine Corps; Department of the Army, Fort Bragg; Art Pence, National Rifle Association of America; Colt Industries Firearms Division; Mary S. Hills of The American Historical Foundation; Smithsonian Institution; WO Tom Sands, Royal Marines; Colour Sergeant Nick Smith, Royal Marines; Major R. Riddell; Rob Lucas-Dean; The Chase Manhattan Bank of New York City; Theodore Roosevelt Collection, Harvard College Library; Kings Mountain National Military Park; Erma-Werke GmbH; Carl Walther GmbH; Heckler & Koch GmbH; Mauser-Werke Oberndorf GmbH; Fabbrica D'Armi Pietro Beretta S.P.A.; Sturm Ruger & Company; Smith & Wesson; American Derringer Corporation; John Norris; Terence Wise of Athena Books; Scicon Limited; and George K. Newark of the Pompadour Gallery, Romford, Essex.

British Library Cataloguing in Publication Data

Newark, Peter
Firefight!
1. Firearms
I. Title
683'.4

ISBN 0-7153-9176-3

© Peter Newark 1989

Typeset by Typesetters (Birmingham) Ltd
Smethwick, West Midlands
Printed in West Germany
by Mohndruck Gmbh
for David & Charles Publishers plc
Brunel House   Newton Abbot   Devon

Distributed in the United States by
Sterling Publishing Co. Inc.,
2, Park Avenue, New York, NY 10016

CONTENTS

British infantry leaving Saxon AT109 armoured personnel carrier. (Photograph by John Norris)

One of a series on musket drill painted by Thomas Rowlandson, 1798. British troops were trained to fire the musket three times a minute.

INTRODUCTION

The purpose of any gun is to do most damage with the least possible expenditure of ammunition. The purpose of tactics is to get the maximum fire effect for the least risk. This book shows how personal firearms have been developed, through history, to improve rate of fire and accuracy, how tactics have developed to make the best use of weapons, and how improved weapons continue to change the nature of modern warfare.

The book is primarily concerned with the man on foot, the infantryman, and with his weapons, his training and his expertise. The individual firepower capability of the modern infantryman would have amazed the musket generals of the Napoleonic period. The regular infantryman of today is armed with an automatic rifle capable of firing up to 940 rounds per minute with a maximum effective range of 800m. His counterpart at Waterloo could manage at best three shots in the same time with his muzzle-loaded flintlock. The Lewis machine gun of World Wars One and Two, requiring two operators, weighing just 27lb and firing 600 rounds per minute to 1,900yd, gave firepower equivalent to fifty World War One riflemen. Today, one infantryman can lay down the same firepower with a gun weighing barely a third as much.

US Airborne soldier armed with the considerably more powerful M16 automatic rifle with 40mm grenade launcher attached. (Photograph by John Norris)

The modern soldier requires accuracy in a firefight, but the musket soldier had little need of such marksmanship, as shooting in volleys at short range was the order of the day. The ultimate desire of all field-commanders, then and now, has always been superiority of fire. The history of firearms is the progression of weapons that can fire faster, farther and more fatally, the quest for more and improved firepower.

The advent of the breech-loading rifle led to swift changes on the battlefield, as it made rapid fire possible and brought in train a sequence of improvements in guns and their ammunition. The breech-loader rifleman is exemplified by the British infantryman of 1914, armed with what many would regard as an exemplary weapon, the bolt-action Short Magazine Lee-Enfield – SMLE.

Typical British 'Tommy' of World War One armed with Lee Enfield Magazine rifle. The regular soldiers of the BEF who marched to war in 1914 were superb riflemen.

Firepower provided by mortar is an essential element of infantry attack and defence. This West German team are working a 120mm heavy mortar. (Photograph by John Norris)

French Army AMX32B tank night-firing its 105mm main armament. (Photograph by John Norris)

British Army Air Corps Gazelle helicopter flying low over Chieftain tanks. The Chieftain is armed with a 120mm gun which is stabilised for accurate firing on the move. Its laser rangefinder can pinpoint a target at many miles' distance and night vision equipment enables the gunner to find his target in darkness, fog or smoke.

The small British Expeditionary Force (BEF) that marched to war in France and Belgium in August 1914 was served by the finest riflemen in modern warfare. These regular soldiers were the twentieth-century equivalent of the medieval longbowmen, trained in marksmanship and rapid fire. In the years leading up to World War One, the British government had ignored the growing importance of the machine gun. In the face of such stubborn myopia, Lt-Colonel N. R. McMahon, Chief Instructor of the School of Musketry at Hythe, decided on a revolutionary plan to train every soldier in marksmanship and rapid fire so that each man would in effect be a 'human machine gun'.

The new rifle training programme was introduced in 1909. By 1914, the British regular army had attained a rate of accurate fire unequalled by any other army – 15–20 rounds per minute using the SMLE. The disciplined firepower of the BEF during the crucial months of August to November 1914 saved the outnumbered force from defeat and changed the course of the war.

The machine gun changed the face of modern warfare. Colonel McMahon's ideal that every infantryman should become 'a human machine gun' has become a reality. The modern infantryman carries an automatic rifle which is a combination of assault rifle and submachine gun with a high cyclic rate of rounds per minute. NATO soldiers use a standard 5.56mm calibre round that has replaced the 7.62mm type ammunition. With the weight of ammunition thus reduced by half, the NATO combat soldier is able to carry twice as much 'ammo' for the same weight.

Automatic rifles can also be fitted with laser devices and an infra-red aiming spotlight which facilitates accurate shooting in darkness. For training purposes, the rifle can be equipped with a low-powered laser projector, aligned with the sight, that fires a pulse of light. If the pulse strikes a human target, it triggers an alarm system on the target-soldier and there is no doubt he has been hit.

The major powers are now investing heavily in the development of new technology and laser weapons and defence systems for deployment in both space and on earth. There is a laser-assisted submachine gun (SMG) developed and manufactured in the United States that is capable of 900 rounds per minute, and, it is claimed, hitting the bull's-eye every time. A pencil-thin laser beam of red light centres on the target and small-calibre bullets are automatically fired along the beam, striking the red dot of the laser on the target.

The American 180 laser SMG was originally conceived as a police weapon to ensure accuracy in picking-off armed criminals in a shoot-out – especially those involving innocent people, or a gunman shielding himself behind a hostage. A number of US police departments have issued special units with the laser SMG.

It is believed that the Israeli commando squad that killed Abu Jihad, the military chief of the Palestine Liberation Organisation, used laser SMGs, fitted with silencers. The Israeli elite unit landed on a Tunisian beach on an April night in 1988 and drove to Abu Jihad's villa in northern Tunis. They stormed the building, killed three armed bodyguards and then confronted Abu Jihad. The Palestinian managed to fire his 9mm pistol at the invaders, but he was cut down by more than seventy bullets in the space of seconds – demonstrating the validity of high rates of fire. One commando evidently had the task of firing at the PLO chief's gun hand. It was practically scythed off by bullets. The commandos escaped without casualties.

French Army mortar team brought into action by jeep-type vehicle. (Photograph by John Norris)

PART ONE EVOLUTION: FROM LONGBOW TO SMLE

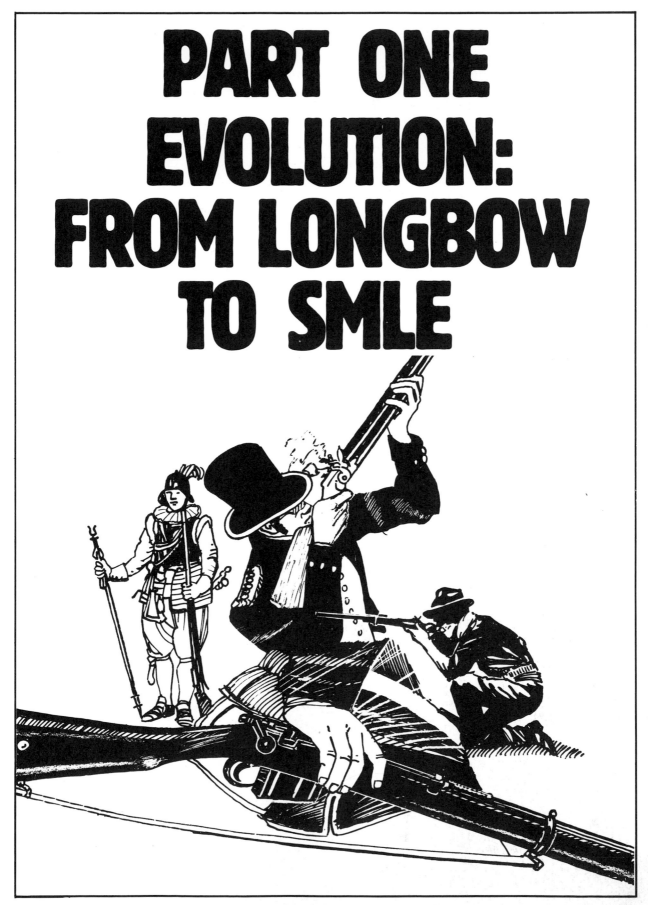

1
MATCHLOCKS AND MUSKETEERS

The death in battle against the Spaniards in 1524 of Pierre du Terrail, Chevalier de Bayard, when his backbone was shattered by a ball from an arquebus, symbolised the irrevocable end of medieval warfare and the beginning of the new age of firearms. Celebrated as the 'knight without fear and without reproach,' Bayard was a shining figure in the pantheon of chivalry, a warrior unvanquished in single combat, a paladin fierce in battle and magnanimous in victory. But his chivalrous spirit did not extend to common handgunners, whom he saw as 'cowardly and base knaves, who would never have dared to have met true soldiers face to face and hand to hand.' This noble French knight ordered all captured arquebusiers to be executed.

Gunfire undermined the archaic feudal system and concluded the military dogma that held the mounted knight to be the principal force in battle. Henceforth, artillery and infantry armed with handguns would decide the destinies of nations. Little wonder that

The death of Chevalier de Bayard, French knight of great renown, mortally wounded by an arquebus bullet while fighting the Spaniards in 1524.

contemporary chroniclers called gunpowder 'the devil's invention'.

Nevertheless, Pierre du Terrail and his knightly brethren had somewhat missed the point of the last two centuries of warfare. Weapons capable of routing an enemy, at ranges well beyond hand-to-hand combat, had already appeared on the battlefield in the form of the bow and arrow.

THE LONGBOW

The longbow was the first weapon to allow real concentrated effective rapid fire. In the hands of English archers, trained from childhood in the use of the weapon, the longbow was a fast-shooting, long-range arm of tremendous impact and importance on the battlefield. At Crecy, Poitiers and Agincourt, the simple longbow humbled the finest of French chivalry. Longbowmen could shoot so quickly that two or three arrows from the same bow could be in flight simultaneously, creating a dark cloud of droning shafts 'falling as thick as snow' that slammed into the armoured knights and horses and transformed a spirited charge into a chaotic and bloody rout.

The bow and arrow had been a prominent weapon of war since ancient times, yet never was so high a standard of archery attained as by the English longbowmen of the fourteenth century. 'A first rate English archer,' a near-contemporary historian wrote, 'who in a single minute was unable to draw and discharge his bow twelve times, with a range of 250 yards, and who in these twelve shots once missed his man, was very lightly esteemed.'

The arbalest or crossbow was the preferred weapon of the French, Italians and Germans. This powerful arm discharged a bolt or quarrel, a short stout shaft with a heavy head or striking point. Although outclassed in rapid fire by the longbow (which could discharge six or more arrows in the time it took a crossbowman to shoot a single bolt), the arbalest was a formidable weapon. It was efficient, accurate and hard-hitting with a greater range than the longbow. The crossbow was finally ousted in European armies by reliable handguns in the sixteenth century.

The longbow, splendid weapon though it was, had the singular disadvantage of requiring long years of practised skill to handle effectively. This constant demand for training and expertise led to the abandonment of the longbow in favour of the handgun and matchlock arquebus. It was a gradual process: the arquebus remained inferior to the longbow in terms of rapid firepower for many years. An archer could shoot off six or more well-aimed arrows in a minute compared to the several minutes required to load and fire one poorly aimed shot from an arquebus. The appearance of effective, accurate and mobile field artillery also rendered the longbow obsolete.

THE FIRST GUNS

We do not know exactly who first composed the explosive mixture of saltpetre, charcoal and sulphur. Some say it was the Chinese or the Arabs, others claim it was first concocted in India. It is most probable that gunpowder originated in China in the twelfth century and was first used in fireworks. In 1986 a stone carving was discovered in a cave in Szechuan province, south-west China, depicting a soldier with a large vase-shaped object from which a flame issued. Was this the first gun? The carving was dated to 1128. Roger Bacon, the English Franciscan friar, recorded a composition for gunpowder in 1242 and described its explosive quality:

> When a portion of this powder, no bigger than a man's finger, is wrapped in a piece of parchment and ignited, it explodes with a blinding flash and a stunning noise.

Guns were first used in Western warfare in the fourteenth century. They were crudely made mortars, huge iron versions of the alchemist's mortar in which gunpowder was mixed with a pestle. These squat, wide-mouthed mortars or bombards hurled iron balls or stones at a high angle of elevation. At first they were of little use as field-pieces, but as siege machines their power of bombardment proved destructive against the walls of the medieval castle. The chronicler Villani mentions the use of guns at the Battle of Crecy in 1346, but these could have done little more than add to the sound of battle.

The first portable handgun dates from the latter half of the fourteenth century and consisted of a short iron tube fixed to a piece of wood and fired by hand, by lighting a charge of gunpowder at a touch-hole.

Jan Zizka

Firearms were first put to intelligent use by Jan Zizka (1370–1424) the hero of Bohemia who led a peasant army of heretics against the Catholic night of the Emperor Sigismund. The one-eyed Zizka protected his ragged soldiers against the armoured knights by constructing waggon forts from farm carts, reinforced with timber and iron and chained together in a circle. The men within these mobile strongholds were armed with crossbows, cannons and handguns.

Austrian bronze mortar of 1583 captured by the Ottoman Turks. On display at the Military Museum, Istanbul.

Handgunners, as depicted in the Rudimentum Noviciorum *published in Lubeck, 1475.*

Zizka won a string of victories. His greatest triumph came at Kutna Mora (now in Czechoslovakia) in 1421. Sigismund had interposed his army between Zizka's mobile camp and the Hussites besieged in the walled town. Under cover of night Zizka unhitched his war waggons and, manning them with hand-gunners, rolled the carts against the Catholic lines, shooting and crushing a way through. Zizka then led his followers to a complete victory over Sigismund's shaken army.

Zizka's peasant handgunners confirmed the new weapon's ignoble use in the minds of the privileged highborn. Such was his contempt for enemy arquebusiers that Gian Paolo Vittelli, the Italian *condottiere*, had all captured handgunners blinded and their hands amputated. But firearms grew in numbers and in military importance. Germany, Italy, France and Spain were foremost in the early development of firearms whilst England had a fine tradition of bowmen skilled in the use of the fast-shooting longbow. Strong opposition against the adoption of military handguns continued in England until the end of the sixteenth century.

THE MATCHLOCK

The matchlock, the earliest form of gunlock mechanism to replace ignition by hand, appeared in the fifteenth century. The matchlock had an S-shaped arm called the serpentine which held a smouldering match (a cord presoaked in saltpetre). Pressure on a trigger brought down the lighted match in contact with the priming powder at the touch-hole. The matchlock was slow to use and often dangerous to the operator, and rain and wind made the weapon useless. A great improvement on the simple technology of the matchlock came in the first quarter of the sixteenth century when the mechanical wheel-lock was invented in Germany.

Matchlock of the seventeenth century. The slow-burning match was held in the curved serpentine and pressure on the trigger lowered it into the priming powder at the touch-hole.

MATCHLOCK (TIME OF WILLIAM III.).

The wheel-lock had a 'cock' (or hammer) holding a piece of pyrites in its jaws. When the trigger was pulled the pyrites made contact with a revolving, serrated steel wheel, thus generating sparks that ignited the priming powder in the pan. The wheel-lock was actuated by a spring wound up by a key. It was a complicated and expensive weapon and, although technically superior to the matchlock, did not replace it but coexisted with it for many years. The wheel-lock was mostly made in pistol form, often highly decorated for noblemen and royalty.

Matchlocks were referred to as the arquebus, harquebus, hackbut and other national variations based on the German *hackenbusche*, or hook gun, probably referring to the hook-shaped butt. The later matchlock musket differs from the arquebus in being much larger and heavier, with a bigger bore, thus requiring a forked rest to support the weapon when firing it. The name musket is the English equivalent of *moschetto*, Italian for the male sparrow hawk, following the tradition of the time in naming cannons and firearms after real or mythical birds and creatures.

The name 'pistol' has several versions of origin. Some say it was named after the Italian town of Pistoia, where the first pistols were allegedly made. Others claim its name stems from pistole, a coin of the time that had the same diameter as the bore of early pistols. Then there is the theory that the name derives from 'pistallo' a pommel. *Pistala*, a Bohemian word for 'pipe' has also been suggested.

MUSKETEERS

By the mid-sixteenth century the pike and musket infantry tactics pioneered by the Spaniards prevailed throughout western Europe. Operating a cumbersome matchlock musket weighing some 20lb (9kg) was a slow business requiring up to thirty drill movements to load and fire it. While doing this the musketeer was protected by pikemen armed with a pike 15ft to 20ft (4.5–6m) long. With the introduction of the ring bayonet at the end of the seventeenth century the musketeer became his own pikeman, able to shoot and stab, and the pike became obsolete.

A sixteenth-century wheel-lock made in Germany. The ball-butt made the pistol easier to draw from a saddle holster. (Photograph courtesy of The National Rifle Association of America)

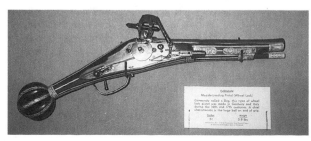

Soldier armed with two wheel-lock pistols. (Illustration from a German book of 1599)

The Battle of Dreux, France, 1562, in the First War of Religion, between Protestant and Catholic forces. Both sides employed pikemen and musketeers. The cavalry were also armed with pistols.

A matchlock musketeer pours gunpowder down the barrel. (Illustration from the manual of arms by Jacob de Gheyn, 1607)

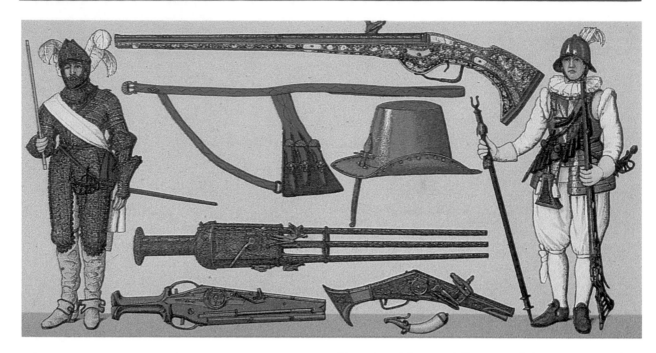

French soldiers and firearms of the seventeenth century.

Balthazar Gerard used a wheel-lock pistol to assassinate the Prince of Orange at Delft in 1584.

The infantry musketeer of the sixteenth and seventeenth centuries was loaded with equipment to serve his weapon. He usually wore a bandolier or cross belt from which hung wooden cylinders, each containing the measured amount of gunpowder for a single shot. Also a large flask of coarse powder for the main charge, a smaller flask of fine priming powder, a leather bullet pouch, and several lengths of slow-burning match, plus his musket rest, sword, and other bits and pieces. In 1619 the following treatise was published in England by Edward Davis:

A soldier must either accustom himself to bear a piece [musket] or pike. If he bears a piece, then must he first learn to hold the same, to accommodate his match between the two foremost fingers and his thumb, and to plant the great end [butt] on his breast with a gallant soldier-like grace . . . let him acquaint himself first with the firing of touch-powder in his [priming] panne, and so by degrees both to shoot off, to bow and to bear up his bodye, and so, consequently, to attain to the level and practice of an assured and serviceable shot, readily to charge [load] and, with comely touch, discharge, making sure at the same instant of his mark, with a quick and vigilant eye.

Matchlocks were taken by the Spanish to conquer the New World of the Americas, and by the colonists of

The musketeer holds the slow-burning match between his fingers in such a manner that he can also use the hand to manipulate the forked rest.

In this de Gheyn illustration the match has been inserted into the serpentine and the musket is ready to be brought into action on the rest.

New England and Virginia. Samuel de Champlain, the French soldier-explorer of Canada and founder of Quebec, relates in his diary how he defeated a tribe of Iroquois in 1609 and captured their fortified village:

> We took, each of us, an arquebus and went ashore. I saw the enemy come out of their barricade to the number of two hundred, in appearance strong and robust men . . . at their head were three chiefs . . . I walked on until I was within thirty yards of the enemy. When I saw them make a move to draw bows upon us, I took aim with my arquebus and shot straight at one of the three chiefs, and with the shot two fell to the ground and one of their companions was wounded and died thereof a little later. I had put four balls into my arquebus . . . As I was reloading one of my companions fired a shot from within the woods which astonished the enemy so much that, seeing their chiefs dead, they lost courage and took flight, abandoning the field and their fort.

Gustavus Adolphus

Gustavus Adolphus (1594–1632) King of Sweden, is regarded as the first modern general for his innovative military organisation and co-operative deployment of the various arms, artillery, musketeers, pikemen and cavalry. The matchlock and the wheel-lock were the firearms of the day. And at a time when most infantrymen were armed with long pikes, Gustavus made the musket a major weapon and increased the number of musketeers in his army. He reduced the weight of the musket so that it could be easily carried and aimed without using a rest. He also adopted the prepared cartridge in which the required measure of powder plus ball (for one shot) were carried in a single container. The cartridge was simple to load and doubled the rate of fire to one round a minute.

Gustavus had the pike shortened to 11ft (3.4m), gave the pikemen lighter armour and trained them to fight with musketeers in formation six ranks deep. Advancing in a central block with two hundred pikemen in the centre, flanked by a hundred muske-teers on each wing, the latter were drilled to maintain continuous fire, shooting by ranks. The front two ranks fired together, then retired through the files, leaving the next two foremost ranks to fire, retire, and so on. By the time the original foremost ranks had

reached the front again they had completed the lengthy reloading procedure and were ready to shoot again.

Later, the musketeers were drilled in salvo shooting to increase firepower. In the salvo three ranks fired simultaneously, the first rank kneeling, the second crouching, the third standing upright. The formation advanced firing volleys until the pikemen made contact with the enemy, who, by then, would be shaken and diminished. Then Gustavus would launch his heavy cavalry for the final, decisive blow. His horsemen were armed with the sword and wheel-lock pistol. Just before contact with the enemy the front ranks of cavalry would discharge their pistols and then go in with the sword; the following ranks kept their pistols holstered for emergency use in the ensuing mêlée.

Gustavus was the first commander to grasp the full importance of field artillery, fusing light guns with infantry and cavalry units. He introduced a light, quick-firing cannon which could be drawn by one horse or three men as opposed to the standard cannon of the day which required twenty horses or more.

Gustavus Adolphus achieved many victories before he died in the Battle of Lutzen, Germany, in 1632

Firearms aided the Spaniards in conquering the Incas of Peru. This old woodcut shows Pizarro taking prisoner Atahualpa, the Inca king, who was executed by his captors in 1533.

Samuel de Champlain and his French arquebusiers attack a fortified Indian village during his exploration of Canada early in the seventeenth century.

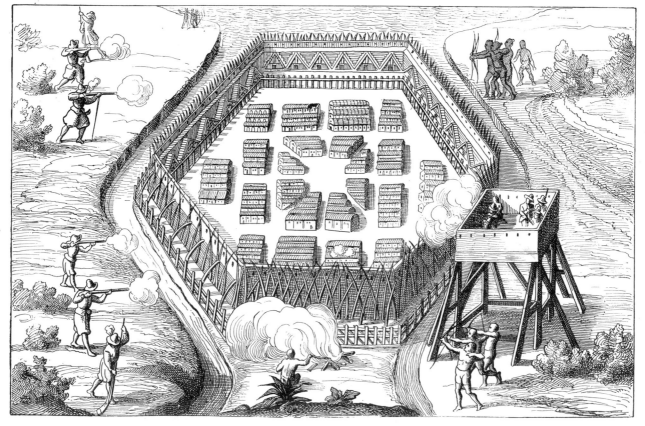

during the Thirty Years War. Ironically, he was killed in a cavalry skirmish while leading a charge. Despite the enormity of the loss of their warrior-king, the Swedes rallied and drove into retreat the enemy forces of the Catholic league, commanded by Count Wallenstein. This was widely regarded as a testimony to the discipline of Gustavus' army. The Swedish system of musket volley or salvo firing was later adopted by Parliament's New Model Army of 1645, during the First Civil War in England.

French Musketeers

In 1600, Henry IV of France created a personal guard of gentlemen armed with the wheel-lock carabine and bestowed the title *Carabiniers du Roi* upon the company. During the reign of Louis XIII (1610–43) the *mousquet* (musket) replaced the carabine and transformed the king's guard into the famous *Mousquetairs*. They wore flamboyant costume: big, floppy boots, cavalier-type hat with large plume, and a blue cloak embroidered with a cross and the royal fleur-de-lis. Richelieu, the king's powerful chief minister, also had a personal company of musketeers who wore red cloaks.

Louis XIV, King of France from 1643 to 1715, reorganised the royal musketeers into two companies: the Grey Musketeers and the Black Musketeers, so called after the colours of their saddle-cloths. They distinguished themselves at the Battle of Steenkerke in 1692 during the War of the Grand Alliance. As part of the *Maison du Roi* cavalry, the Musketeers launched several spirited counter-attacks against the allied force of William of Orange, suffering heavy casualties in driving William into retreat. The *Mousquetairs* were disbanded when Napoleon came to power.

THE SNAPHAUNCE

The next significant evolutionary step in the development of firearms came with an improved system of spark ignition; a simpler, more reliable method to replace the expensive and complicated wheel-lock.

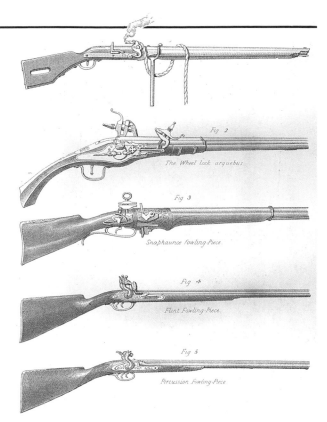

Small arms progression, from the matchlock to the percussion system.

Enter the snaphaunce (snaphance, snaplock) in the middle of the sixteenth century. The snaphaunce, the earliest form of the flintlock system, consisted of a jawed cock or hammer that gripped a sharpened piece of flint. On pressing the trigger the cock snapped forward and the flint struck a steel (frizzen), thus generating sparks into the powder in the priming pan, and via a touch-hole, detonated the main charge.

The snaphaunce was a technological breakthrough in that it was far superior to the matchlock, and a better system and cheaper to produce (and repair) than the wheel-lock. A French gunmaker, Marin le Bourgeoys, improved and refined the snaphaunce and, in the first quarter of the seventeenth century, the flintlock proper came into use. This differed from the snaphaunce in various mechanical additions inside the lock, and, most importantly, the frizzen was made to combine the function of steel and priming pan cover. The frizzen was kept in place by a spring mounted on the lock exterior. When the flint struck the frizzen and produced sparks, the frizzen simultaneously snapped forward, uncovering the pan.

The flintlock dominated the industry until the invention of the percussion system (1807) and its general adoption towards the middle of the nineteenth century.

Gustavus Adolphus, martial king of Sweden and innovative advocate of firepower, was killed in a cavalry clash during the Battle of Lutzen, 1632.

2
FLINTLOCK
FIRE

While the crash and carnage of the Battle of Trafalgar raged below, French sharpshooters in the high fighting tops of the warship *Redoutable* picked off the enemy officers they could spot on the smoke-laden, chaotic decks of HMS *Victory*. The ships were grinding sides and blasting each other with broadsides. One officer, his chest resplendent in gleaming orders of chivalry, caught the eye of a French marksman in the mizzentop. He fired his flintlock musket at the distinctive but slight figure of Admiral Lord Nelson, who sank to his knees.

'They have done for me at last, Hardy,' he said to his captain, who stooped over him. 'My backbone is shot through.'

The musket ball had passed through his left shoulder, struck down through his chest and lodged in the spine. Dying, he was carried below to the surgeon in the cockpit. The *Redoutable* struck her colours (surrendered) some fifteen minutes after the fatal shot. Nelson, in great agony, lived long enough to know he had won the day at Cape Trafalgar, 21 October 1805, against the combined French and Spanish fleets.

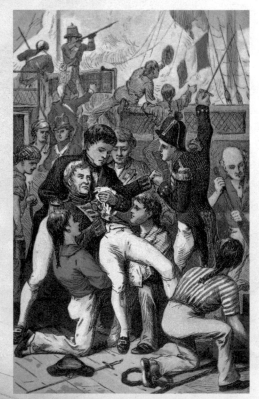

Nelson mortally wounded during the Battle of Trafalgar, struck down by a French sharpshooter.

It is not clear exactly who killed Nelson. There are several versions. Southey in his *Life of Nelson* (1813) gives the following account:

It was not long before there were only two Frenchmen left alive in the mizzentop of the *Redoutable*. One of them was the man who had given [Nelson] the fatal wound. He did not live to boast of what he had done. An old quartermaster had seen him fire and easily recognised him, because he wore a glazed cocked hat and white frock. This quartermaster and two midshipmen, Mr Collingwood and Mr Pollard, were the only persons left on the *Victory*'s poop; the two midshipmen kept firing at the top and he supplied them with cartridges. One of the Frenchmen, attempting to make his escape down the rigging, was shot by Mr Pollard and fell on the poop.

The old quartermaster, as he cried out, 'That's he, that's he' [who had shot Nelson], and pointed at the other Frenchman, received a shot in the mouth and fell dead. Both midshipmen then fired at the same time and the fellow dropped in the top. When they took possession of the prize, they went into the mizzentop and found him dead with one ball through the head, and another through the breast.

The flintlock system of igniting the gunpowder in a musket or pistol, developed in France about 1630–40, was an improvement on the earlier snaplock or snaphaunce method that employed a flint striking steel to produce sparks. The flintlock comprised a flint gripped in the jaws of a cock. On pulling the trigger the cock sprang forward and the flint struck the steel frizzen, throwing sparks into the priming pan powder and thus igniting, by way of a vent or touch-hole, the main charge in the barrel and firing off the ball. In the classic flintlock the falling cock not only struck the sparks but simultaneously uncovered the priming pan which, up to that moment, had been covered and protected against accidental dispersion (of the priming powder) and the weather.

THE 'BROWN BESS' MUSKET

The introduction of the flintlock system marks the beginning of the age of simple and reliable firearms that could be produced in large numbers. The flintlock served as the chief, if not the sole means of musket and pistol ignition for two centuries. A celebrated military musket was the British 'Brown Bess' carried by the world-tramping redcoats for more than a hundred years. Rudyard Kipling eulogised the weapon in 'Brown Bess':

In the days of lace-ruffles, perukes and brocade
  Brown Bess was a partner whom none could
    despise –
An out-spoken, flinty-lipped, brazen-faced jade,
  With a habit of looking men straight in the eyes –
At Blenheim and Ramillies fops would confess
  They were pierced to the heart by the charms of
    Brown Bess . . .

Flintlock of about 1790 showing the steel frizzen in place covering the priming pan.

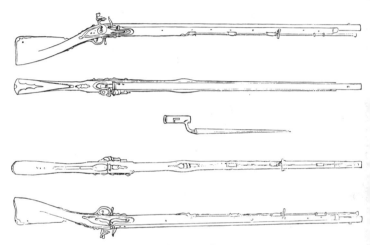

The British Army 'Brown Bess' of 1786.

So she followed her redcoats, whatever they did,
  From the heights of Quebec to the plains of Assaye,
From Gibraltar to Acre, Cape Town to Madrid,
  And nothing about her was changed on the way;
(But most of the Empire which now we possess
Was won through those years by old-fashioned
  Brown Bess) . . .

'Brown Bess' is the generic name for a long line of standard issue flintlock smooth-bore muskets, approved by the Board of Ordnance, that served as the main weapon of the British Army from the 1730s to the 1830s. The 'Brown Bess' progressed through the Long Land Pattern, Short Land Pattern, the India Pattern, and the New Land Pattern; the Land Pattern differed somewhat from the Sea Service musket. The most common model was the India Pattern, of which three million were produced between 1793 and the end of 1815.

The origin of the 'Brown Bess' nickname is not clear. It could well be that the 'Brown' came from the 'browning' process employed to dull and protect the barrel against corrosion, and the 'Bess' from 'buss' a corruption of the German *buchse*, meaning gun, as used in 'arquebus' and 'blunderbuss'. With the

Redcoat firepower at the Battle of Fontenoy, 1745.

smooth-bore musket, the lead ball fitted loosely in the barrel and much of the explosive force of the charge was wasted; therefore shooting was very inaccurate. Colonel George Hanger, a marksman and firearms authority, published the following comments in 1814:

> A soldier's musket, if not exceedingly ill-bored (as many are), will strike the figure of a man at 80 yards; it may even at a hundred; but a soldier must be very unfortunate indeed who shall be wounded by a common musket at 150 yards . . . and as to firing at a man at 200 yards, you may as well fire at the moon . . . I do maintain and will prove, whenever called on, that no man was ever killed at 200 yards by a common soldier's musket, by the person who aimed at him.

The battle-winning firepower of the 'Brown Bess' came in disciplined volleys; a wall of rapid fire delivered at short range by solid ranks or squares of infantry against an enemy advancing en masse. Trained redcoats, carrying sixty prepared cartridges in a pouch, could fire two or three shots a minute, sometimes more. The cartridge, a paper tube containing the required amount of powder and ball, was sealed by a twisted end. To load, the twisted end was bitten off and a little powder pinched into the priming pan, which was then closed. The rest of the powder and the ball were rammed home into the barrel. The

flintlock was pulled back to full cock and the musket was presented and fired.

'Brown Bess' demonstrated her devastating firepower at Waterloo in 1815. Wrote Lord Hill, commander of the 2nd Corps:

> For upwards of an hour our squares were surrounded by the elite of the French cavalry. They gallantly stood within forty paces of us, unable to leap over the bristling line of bayonets, unwilling to retire, and determined never to surrender. Hundreds of them were dropping in all directions from our murderous fire.

Foy, the French general, paid tribute to the stalwart redcoats. 'Neither the bullets of the Imperial Guard nor the hitherto victorious French cavalry could break the immovable British infantry. One would have been inclined to believe that they had taken root to the ground.'

THE 'CHARLEVILLE' MUSKET

The French rival of 'Brown Bess,' on many battlefields, was the standard infantry musket produced by the government arms factories at St Etienne, Tulle, Charleville, and Mauberge. The various flintlock muskets from these plants served the French Army from 1717 until long after Waterloo. These weapons are known to gun collectors as 'Charleville' muskets. The French calibre of .69in (17.47mm) was slightly

Shooting the Popinjay, a mark in the shape of a bird, a popular seventeenth-century sport.

A French sergeant dressing an immaculate volley with the aid of a partisan staff-weapon in the eighteenth century.

smaller than the 'Brown Bess' and the barrel was better made; the ball had a closer fit in the bore, thus achieving greater accuracy and distance than the British muskets.

In spite of the superior quality of the French musket over the 'Brown Bess' in the Napoleonic Wars it was not employed effectively owing to the differing tactics of the protagonists. The French usually attacked, pressing the advance with spirited elan at bayonet point, and were successful against armies not as disciplined or as well-drilled in rapid fire as the British infantry, who, formed in defensive ranks or squares, blasted such onslaughts into retreat. For outstanding feats of valour Napoleon presented his soldiers with *Fusils d'Honneur*, special muskets adorned with a silver plaque on the butt inscribed with the man's name, his brave deed and the date.

The French Model of 1763 is often referred to by collectors as the 'Lafayette' musket because the French general and nobleman of that name supplied several thousand of the 1763, at his own expense, to the rebel colonists fighting the British during the American Revolution. The US Musket Model 1795, the first flintlock firearm to be made in a US Armoury (at Springfield), was closely based on the French pattern 1763. Although the eighty thousand French muskets used against the British in the War of Independence contributed to the winning of American freedom, the so-called 'Kentucky' rifle deserves a special commendation for its sharp-shooting service in the great struggle.

THE 'KENTUCKY' RIFLE

The 'Kentucky' rifle, a native American original, fashioned to meet the requirements of the backwoods hunter, evolved from the heavy jaeger (hunting) rifle of big calibre used by the German and Swiss immigrants to Pennsylvania in the late seventeenth century. The Germans and the Swiss transplanted their gunmaking skills to Pennsylvania and places like Lancaster, York and Hagerstown became renowned for quality handmade rifles. The German-

French cavalryman of 1766 armed with sabre, a brace of pistols and a carbine. Illustration from *The Uniforms of the King's Household Troops and all the French Regiments* by De Monsigny.

An American soldier of the War of Independence priming the pan of his French musket.

(above) *French flintlock pistol, circa 1810, with the distinctive half-stock under the barrel, as opposed to the English-style full stock.*

(below) *An eighteenth-century blunderbuss, popular short-range defence weapon with householders and stagecoach guards.*

DEATH OF A GENERAL

Colonel George Hanger was on active service during the War of Independence with the Hessian Jaegers and Tarleton's Legion. He was a noted authority on firearms and a fervent advocate of a light infantry role which was made possible by improved firearms. He was full of praise for the ability of the rebel riflemen to use the ground and their rifles. He wrote: 'I never in my life saw better rifles (or men who shot better) than those made in America.'

Hanger himself was shot at by a rifleman at 400yd (365m) distance. The bullet passed between him and another officer and killed the horse of a bugler directly behind Hanger. Hanger had the sense to move to a safer position.

The maximum effective range of the 'Brown Bess' was between 80 and 90yd (75–80m), with a maximum accurate range by individuals of just over 100yd, but the maximum range at which the average Continental American infantryman could achieve accuracy with his rifle was 150yd. Individual performances with the American weapon were considerably greater. Hanger maintained that 'provided an American rifleman was to get a perfect aim at 300yd (275m) at me standing still, he most undoubtedly would hit me, unless it was a very windy day.'

Colonel George Hanger was right, and rifleman Timothy Murphy proved him right by shooting dead General Simon Fraser at just that range. Murphy was a legendary rifleman from Pennsylvania whose skilled marksmanship helped to bring about a British defeat. The 'Kentucky' rifle was his natural weapon. Murphy had an unusual double-barrelled 'Kentucky,' with an 'over and under' pair of barrels secured on an axle at the breech end. After firing the upper

Pennsylvania rifleman Timothy Murphy, up in a tree, shoots General Simon Fraser during the Saratoga campaign, October 1777.
(Painting by H. Charles McBarron, courtesy of US Army)

barrel, and releasing a spring catch, both barrels were revolved by hand until the lower one was on top, where it was secured ready to fire.

Murphy was a member of the special rifle corps formed in April 1777 under the command of Colonel Daniel Morgan, and in which sharpshooters used their own long rifles. The corps took part in the battle for Saratoga in October 1777. During the battle, the brave and inspiring action of General Simon Fraser, commanding the British right, brought him to the special attention of Colonel Morgan, who was advised to dispose of him as a matter of the greatest urgency. Morgan instructed a party of his sharpshooters, which included Murphy, to carry out the task: 'See that gallant officer on the grey horse. That is General Fraser. I respect him – but it is necessary that he should die.'

The riflemen were in the edge of a wood. The shot could be made from no closer than 300yd (275m) range, and Murphy's aim was put to the test. His rifle was already loaded. He climbed a tree and rested his rifle on a branch. Murphy's elevation from the tree gave him a clear view of Fraser and a surer trajectory. His heartbeat raced as he took careful aim on the general and squeezed the trigger. The hammer flashed the priming powder, the main charge crashed. Through the clearing smoke, Murphy saw the mortally wounded Fraser slump from his horse.

The general's death led to the British retreat and surrender at Saratoga – a disaster for Britain. The defeat of a regular British army in America was a serious blow to British reputation and a firm bolster for rebel morale. It was a turning point in the war.

'Kentucky' rifles are popular with black-powder shooters of today. Here we see a fine group of modern Kentucky-style muzzleloaders at a meeting at Brady, Texas.

'Kentucky' rifle with characteristic ornamental patchbox lid. The hinged lid contained greased leather patches that were wrapped round each rifle ball to ensure a tight fit in the barrel.

American colonists slimmed down the traditional jaeger and gave it extra length and a smaller bore, the resulting weapon being an instrument of beauty, reliability and accuracy. The rifled bore, as opposed to the smoothbore, imparted a twist to the bullet on leaving the barrel and ensured greater accuracy, velocity and range. The Pennsylvania long rifle became the favourite weapon of frontiersmen and hunters of colonial America.

Although the weapon originated in Pennsylvania, its popular name of 'Kentucky' rifle came into being through its association with Daniel Boone, Davy Crockett and others who pioneered the Kentucky country. Kentucky and Tennessee riflemen helped Andrew Jackson defeat the British in the Battle of New Orleans on 8 January 1815 by picking off the officers leading and directing the redcoats. The ballad entitled 'The Hunters of Kentucky; or The Battle of New Orleans' did much to establish the fame and the name of the long rifle. Here is part of it:

But Jackson he was wide awake,
   And wasn't scar'd at trifles,
For well he knew what aim we take
   With our Kentucky rifles.
So he led us up to a cyprus swamp,
   The ground was low and mucky,
There stood John Bull in martial pomp,
   And here was old Kentucky.

The small bore of the long rifle, mostly .40in–.45in (11.43mm) calibre, required less powder and lead. The lead ball was wrapped in a greased leather or linen patch and rammed down the muzzle, the patch imparting a tight fit to the ball, thus ensuring greater muzzle velocity. The patches were kept in a patchbox carved into the rifle's butt and covered with a hinged metal lid, often extravagantly designed, a distinctive feature of the Pennsylvania-Kentucky rifle. Also, a fine priming powder was used (coarse grain for the main charge) which gave faster, surer ignition.

The American long rifle was deadly accurate at 100yd and could kill at 300yd.

When reports got back to London about the native American 'wonder weapon' that could kill at 300yd, the army was instructed to capture a 'specimen' sharpshooter complete with long rifle and ship him to England. Thus it was that Corporal Walter Crouse of York County, Pennsylvania, found himself in London as a privileged prisoner of war giving private and public demonstrations of his shooting prowess. His marksmanship so impressed King George III that he ordered the employment of German Hessian troops armed with rifles to aid his redcoats in America. But the Hessian guns were the old style, heavy, slow-loading type from which the Pennsylvania long rifle had evolved, and the five thousand Hessian riflemen proved of little value in the war.

THE FERGUSON RIFLE

A weapon that might have had a significant effect on the outcome of the American Revolution was the Ferguson rifle, which not only equalled the range and accuracy of the Pennsylvania-type long rifle, but had the superior advantage of being a breech-loader. This rifle, remarkable for its time, was developed by

DAVY Crockett, frontiersman folk hero, holding his 'Kentucky' rifle named 'Betsey'. In the winter of 1825–6 he hunted and shot fifty-eight bears.

Scotsman Patrick Ferguson, a former army captain and a marksman of renown. He based his successful breech-loading system on the earlier works of the Frenchman Chaumette and the Englishman John Warsop. Aided by London gunmaker Durs Egg, Ferguson perfected a prototype rifle and demonstrated its capabilities at a Board of Ordnance trial at Woolwich. The *Annual Register* recorded the event:

> On the 1st June 1776, he [Ferguson] made some experiments at Woolwich, before Lord Viscount Townsend, Lord Amherst, General Harvey . . . and several other officers with the rifle gun on a new construction, which astonished all beholders. The like had never been done with any other small arms. Notwithstanding a heavy rain and the high wind, he fired during the space of five minutes at the rate of four shots a minute, at a target two hundred yards distance. He next fired six shots in one minute, and also fired (while advancing at the rate of four miles an hour) four times in a minute . . .

Displaying the sense of a showman, Ferguson then poured a bottle of water into the priming pan and down the barrel to thoroughly wet the powder and ball; he then removed the damp powder, leaving the ball in the breech, recharged with fresh powder and fired the rifle without any trouble. This entire experiment took thirty seconds.

> Lastly, he hit the bull's eye lying on his back on the ground, incredible as it may seem to many, considering the variations of the wind and the wetness of the weather. He only missed the target three times during the whole course of the experiments.

As a result of this spectacular demonstration, and another in front of King George III, the Board of Ordnance placed a small initial order for one hundred Ferguson rifles. The Scot was granted a patent for his weapon in December 1776. In March 1777, Ferguson landed in New York with his hundred rifles and a special corps of riflemen. His men first saw action in the battle of Brandywine, where the rifle corps suffered heavy casualties; Ferguson himself had his right elbow shattered by a bullet.

While carrying out reconnaissance during the battle of Brandywine, Ferguson was concealed in some brush when a senior American officer accompanied by a French hussar rode into view. The Scottish marksman raised his rifle and got the American in his sights . . . but did not fire.

Very soon after this incident Ferguson discovered from a captured American soldier that the officer he had lined up in his sights was none other than George Washington! If Ferguson had been more ruthless he could have changed the outcome of the war, indeed the course of history.

The death of Sir Edward Pakenham in the Battle of New Orleans, January 1815. He was most probably shot by a 'Kentucky' rifle.

Promoted lieutenant-colonel, Ferguson led a large force into South Carolina, burning and destroying everything in his path, gaining the title 'Butcher of the Carolinas'. The Americans finally brought Ferguson to bay on a timbered hill called Kings Mountain. Brave as ever, Ferguson rode among his men to encourage them in the desperate fight. Fully exposed to the enemy, he was killed, and with him died the Ferguson rifle.

His revolutionary weapon, if produced in sufficient numbers, could have been a war winner. It might have replaced the 'Brown Bess'. But the hidebound British generals were not interested in sophisticated new rifles. They believed that simple musket volleys and bayonet charges won battles. The first Earl Grey, for example, was dubbed the 'No-flint General' from his common practice of ordering his men to take the flints out of their muskets, thus confining them to the use of the bayonet.

A Ferguson military rifle is a *rara avis* in the gun-collecting field today. Virtually all the original hundred rifles taken to America have disappeared. The Smithsonian Institution have one, the Morristown National Historical Park have another, and a third is in the West Point Museum. Perhaps others reside in private collections not known to the public.

The British Army ignored a grand opportunity in not adopting and developing the Ferguson. More than eighty-five years would pass before another breech-loading rifle, the Snider-Enfield of 1865, came into service with the British soldier.

General Andrew Jackson, mounted in the foreground, directs the American victory over the British in the Battle of New Orleans, 1815. (Painting by H. Charles McBarron, courtesy of US Army)

3
DUELLING DAYS

It has a strange, quick jar upon the ear,
  That cocking of a pistol, when you know
A moment more will bring the sight to bear
  Upon your person, twelve yards off or so.
                                        Byron

On a May morning in 1806 General Andrew Jackson faced Charles Dickinson in a pistol duel at the deadly distance of eight paces. Jackson was exceptionally brave and a good shot, but his opponent was celebrated as the best marksman in Tennessee and a feared duellist. Jackson also knew that at eight paces Dickinson could put four bullets into a silver dollar. But the general's honour demanded satisfaction at pistol point. He had challenged Dickinson for having slandered his wife, whom he adored 'with a romantic tenderness and strength surpassing the dream of fiction.'

Jackson was forty years old, tall, slim and wiry, tough as 'Old Hickory,' his nickname. It was agreed between both parties, the principals and their seconds, that pistols would be held downwards and, on the given signal, each man would fire as he pleased. Jackson had decided to hold his fire, that is, let the crackshot Dickinson shoot first. When he informed General Overton, his second, of this intention, Overton exclaimed: 'Hickory, if you hold your fire you'll probably not live to pull the trigger!'

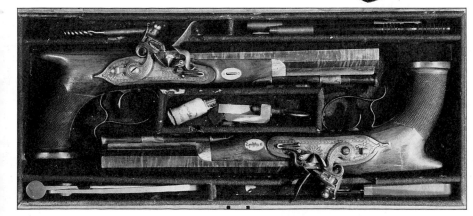

London-made flintlock duelling pistols owned by Andrew Jackson. Note the fashionable saw-type butt. (Photograph courtesy of The Smithsonian Institution)

Jackson replied, 'I know it, but I must have time to get a line on him. I'll take the chance. My luck's always good.'

On the signal Dickinson immediately fired at the long, gaunt figure in the loose-fitting coat. A puff of dust flew from Jackson's breast, indicating a hit in the area of the heart. The general swayed only slightly and stood rooted to the spot. Dickinson stared with amazement at the upright Jackson, who now levelled his pistol. 'Great God, have I missed him?' gasped Dickinson, and stepped back. At this Overton snapped: 'Back on your mark, sir!' He did so, turning his face away from his vengeful adversary. Jackson took careful aim at the man who had insulted his beloved wife and fired. Dickinson fell mortally wounded.

Attempt on General Jackson's life.

Andrew Jackson became US President in 1829. In 1835 an assassin fired a pistol at Jackson at close range. The percussion cap exploded but failed to discharge the bullet. The assassin then fired a second pistol and this also misfired. Jackson pursued the man and saw him secured. When the pistols were examined they were found to be in excellent order, containing both bullet and high-grade gunpowder. How the caps could have detonated without firing the main charge is still a mystery.

The duel between the Duke of Wellington and Lord Winchilsea in 1829. Although the Duke was opposed to duelling, honour forced him to challenge Winchilsea over an alleged insult. Both deliberately fired wide. Winchilsea apologised and honour was satisfied.

As Jackson walked slowly away from the scene, Overton realised that his friend had been hit (the bullet had broken two ribs), but Jackson made little of the injury, instructing Overton not to say a word about it. Such was his rancour towards Dickinson that he wanted him to die in the belief that the finest shot in Tennessee had missed his man at eight paces. Jackson soon recovered and maintained that so fixed was his resolution at the duel that 'I should have killed him even had he shot me through the brain.'

Jackson went on to become the hero of the Battle of New Orleans (1815) and in 1829 he took office as the seventh President of the United States. Later in the century an authority on duelling commented on the subject of his duel with Dickinson:

There is one feature about this duel that seems a little peculiar, and that is that General Jackson, who was a very spare man in his person, should have been dressed in a loose-fitting gown or coat, so that his antagonist could not readily tell the location of his body.

Dickinson aimed right; and if Jackson's body had been where Dickinson supposed it was, and where, perhaps the *code duello* would say it ought to have been, there is no just reason to doubt that Jackson would at that time have 'passed in his checks' . . .

Having dressed in a manner to deceive Dickinson as to the precise location of his body [heart], and having received Dickinson's bullet without any serious injury, it was not a just and fair thing in Jackson afterwards to take deliberate aim at Dickinson and kill him.

But then Jackson was a backwoods gentleman, a fighter, a born survivor, not a foolhardy gentleman of the drawing-room type, ready and willing to throw his life away. Duelling with pistols in the formal manner, that is, between gentlemen of equal status, and attended by seconds, flourished in Europe and the United States from about 1770 to 1870, a century

in which a gentleman's honour was his most prized possession; a delicate flower easily bruised. Any insult, real or imagined, petty or malicious, could only be wiped out by challenging the perpetrator to a duel with swords or pistols.

THE DUELLING CODE

If the man 'called out' refused the challenge then he was considered a coward and was ostracised by the society he held so dear. Gentlemen fought duels to preserve their honour, to show they had courage, and some for the excitement of the moment. Death was disregarded when personal esteem was at stake.

Such was the social pressure regarding duelling that many prominent figures, although opposed to the custom, were nevertheless lured into its eristic web. The Duke of Wellington, Charles James Fox, and the American Alexander Hamilton were against duelling, yet the ethics of honour induced them to take up pistols to settle a matter that could not be resolved any other way.

French and Italians mostly duelled with blades. Prussians preferred the sabre. The English, Irish, and the Americans favoured the more deadly satisfaction offered by the pistol. It was in Ireland, a veritable hotbed of duelling, that a group of gentlemen at Clonmel Summer Assizes in 1777 drew up a code of conduct, the *Code Duello*, to govern the spreading social craze and bring recognised order to the occasion. Here is an extract from the code:

All imputations of cheating at play, races, etc., to be considered equivalent to a blow, but may be reconciled after one shot, on admitting their falsehood and begging pardon publicly . . .

No dumb firing or firing in the air is admissible in any case. The challenger ought not to have challenged without receiving offence, and the challenged [party] ought, if he gave offence, to have made an apology before he came on the ground; therefore children's play must be dishonourable and is accordingly prohibited.

Seconds to be of equal rank in society with the principals they attend . . . The challenged has the right to choose his own weapons unless the challenger gives his honour he is no swordsman, after which, however, he cannot decline any second species of weapon proposed by the challenged. The challenged chooses the ground, the challenger chooses the distance, the seconds fix the time and terms of firing . . .

The seconds load in presence of each other, unless they give their mutual honours that they have charged smooth and single [smooth-bore pistols and a single bullet]. Firing may be regulated first by signal; secondly by word of command; or thirdly at pleasure, as may be agreeable to the parties . . .

A cased pair of flintlock duellers by the celebrated London gunsmith Robert Wogdon. (Photograph courtesy of Christie's South Kensington Ltd)

In all cases a misfire is equivalent to a shot. Seconds are bound' to attempt a reconciliation before the meeting takes place, or after sufficient firing or hits as specified. Any wound sufficient to agitate the nerves and necessarily make the hand shake must end the business for the day.

There were, however, a number of different codes drawn up over the following years and rules varied somewhat. The most common arrangement in duelling countries was the face-to-face confrontation at an agreed distance, usually ten to fifteen paces. Books were published advising a duellist how to prepare himself for the dangerous meeting, how to present himself, and the proper stance to adopt on the ground. An experienced duellist showed only his side to his opponent, with his outstretched (pistol) arm shielding his chest, and with his stomach drawn tightly in. He might also bury his chin into his shoulder. Such a posture presented the smallest target area possible. He would also wear dark clothes with cloth buttons, so that his adversary could not draw a bead on a gleaming metal button.

A veteran duellist known as 'Fighting' Fitzgerald could reduce his height by five or six inches. 'His plan was to bend his head over his body until the upper portion of him resembled a bow,' explained William Douglas in *Duelling Days in the Army* (1887). 'His right hand and arm were held in front of his head in such a manner that a ball would have to pan all up his arm before it touched a vulnerable part.' Smooth-bore pistols were loaded with ball, not pointed bullets. In *The Art of Duelling*, published in 1836, the anonymous author counsels the reader on being wounded, and on dying:

I cannot impress upon an individual too strongly the propriety of remaining perfectly calm and collected when hit; he must not allow himself to be alarmed or confused; but summoning up all his resolution, treat the matter coolly; and if he dies, go off with as good a grace as possible.

An eighteenth-century duel.

Some reluctant duellists of large size were completely blasé about adopting the proper stance. When the rotund politician Charles James Fox met William Adam at Hyde Park, London, in 1779, Fox was advised by his second to stand sideways in the recommended manner. 'To what purpose, sir?' Fox remarked. 'I'm as thick one way as the other!' Adam wounded Fox, but not seriously, and the gallant Fox fired into the air. He used his injury to good political effect. The cause of the duel had been Fox's criticism of the poor quality of government gunpowder. On his return to Parliament, Fox delivered the following shot at the Opposition: 'Yes, I am lucky to be alive – lucky that Mr Adam's pistols were charged with government powder!'

DUELLING PISTOLS

For a gentleman of strong opinions to move in a volatile duelling society it was prudent of him to mind his manners, guard his tongue, and to 'know his pistols.' There were shooting galleries where one could practise, and establishments where instruction was given by pistol experts. The author of *The Art of Duelling* (1836) certainly 'knew his pistols':

The pistols I prefer for duelling should measure ten inches in length in the barrels . . . furnished with percussion locks of delicate workmanship fitted into a firm stock bent into a curve that will fit the hand comfortably. To each barrel should

Mardon's Shooting Gallery, 94 Pall Mall, London, circa 1825–30. Experienced duellists and army officers found it necessary to maintain their marksmanship by regular practice.

be affixed two sights, one in the breech, carefully set for the centre, and the second about half an inch from the muzzle. I do not approve of silver sights for they are apt, when the sun glances on them, to dazzle and deceive the eye. Those of blued steel are best. The best pistol locks I have seen have been manufactured by Purdey in Oxford Street [London].

The French and British, especially the latter, were acknowledged as the finest makers of duelling pistols. The art of the gunsmith reached a peak of perfection in the manufacture of flintlock and percussion duellers. A top class duelling pistol was a remarkable piece of functional design and engineering; a handsome instrument of death that could 'inflict a mortal wound at more than forty yards.' In a period when the common flintlock pistol was notoriously inaccurate, the skilfully made dueller was deadly accurate and so well balanced that one needed only to raise it to be right on target.

Made in matched pairs, duelling pistols were sold in a case of fine quality wood, with fitted compartments to hold the necessary accessories. The general characteristics of a duelling pistol are a heavy steel barrel, very often octagonal in shape, a deeply incised butt to ensure a firm grip and steady aim, a small bead foresight and a vee backsight. The barrel and metal fittings are usually dulled with a browning finish in order not to reflect the light. Refinements included gold or platinum-lined flashpan and touch-hole to eliminate corrosion, a hair trigger so delicately set that only slight pressure was required to fire the weapon, and an additional spur on the trigger guard to assist a nervous hand and to counter any tendency of the barrel to rise on firing. Flintlock duellers were fully stocked, with the wood underpart extending the full length of the barrel. Later percussion pistols were mostly half stocked.

Among the celebrated English gunmakers of duelling pistols were the London establishments of Robert Wogdon, Joseph and John Manton, H. W. Mortimer, Durs Egg, James Purdey, John Nock and Henry Twigg. Birmingham boasted the skill of Westley Richards, and Dublin had the Rigby family. In France, Nicholas Boutet reigned supreme as *Arquebusier du Roi* at Versailles, and in Napoleon's time Le Page of Paris, *Arquebusier de l'Empereur*. Robert Wogdon's cased pistols were so popular between 1780–90 that when a quarrel was settled outside the law on the duelling ground, it was often referred to as a 'Wogdon's Case'. *Stanzas on Duelling*, published in 1782, contained the following lines:

> Hail Wogdon, Patron of that leaden death
>   Which waits alike the bully and the brave
> As well might Art recall departed breath
>   As any artifice your victims save.

Sir Jonah Barrington, an Irish judge, was an experienced duellist and in *Personal Sketches of His Own Times*, published in 1827, he describes his first duel, with Richard Daly of Galway:

At 7am with a cold wind and sleet, I set out with my second, the brother of Sir Edward Crosby, for the field of Donnybrook Fair, having taken some good chocolate and a plentiful draught of cherry brandy to keep out the cold. On arriving we saw my antagonist and his second, Jack Patterson, nephew of the Chief Justice, already on the ground . . .

Daly was something of a dandy, called a 'macaroni' in those days. On this occasion, he wore a pea-green coat, a large tucker (a frilled, falling collar of linen or lace), a three-cocked hat with a gold button loop and tassels, and silk stockings. His tucker was adorned with a diamond brooch. Barrington's second softly advised him 'Never aim at the head or heels. Hip the

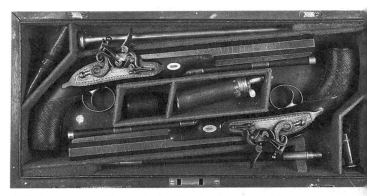

A fine brace of flintlock duellers constructed by John Manton of London. (Photograph courtesy of Christie's South Kensington Ltd)

Cased percussion duellers by Westley Richards of Birmingham, England.

The London-made Wogdon pistols used in the Burr-Hamilton duel. It is interesting to see that one of these flintlock pistols was later converted to percussion. (Photograph courtesy of The Chase Manhattan Archives)

macaroni! The hip forever my boy!' The duellists stood nine paces apart. Barrington continues:

Daly presented his pistol instantly but gave me most gallantly a full front. I let fly without a moment's delay. Daly staggered back two or three steps, put his hand to his breast and cried: 'I'm hit, Sir!' He did not fire. We opened his waistcoast and a black spot, the size of a crown piece with a little blood, appeared directly over his breast bone. The ball had not penetrated, but his brooch had been broken and a piece of the setting was sticking fast in the bone. Daly put his cambric handkerchief to his breast and bowed. I returned his salute and we parted without conversation or ceremony.

Another duel with a strange ending took place in Paris between two of Napoleon's generals, Bonnet and Ornano, the latter being renowned for his marksmanship. Bonnet shot first with no effect. Ornano took careful aim, fired, and was surprised, if not amazed to see his adversary still standing, apparently unjurt. The reason was soon discovered when Bonnet removed a buckled five-franc coin from his breast pocket. '*Morbleu!*' remarked Ornano. 'You have invested your money most fortunately.' When Lord George Germaine met George Johnstone in London in 1770, the latter's bullet shattered Germaine's pistol in his hand, and both left the field unhurt.

HONOUR AND THE LAW

The law condemned duelling but could not prevent it from taking place. However, if a duel proved fatal the surviving party could be charged with murder. Captain Macnamara stood trial for murder in 1803, having killed Colonel Montgomery in a duel resulting from a fight between their dogs in Hyde Park, London. He made a forceful speech in defence of his action and his honour:

I am a captain of the British Navy. My character you can hear from others. But to maintain my character in that situation I must be respected. When called upon to lead others into honourable danger, I must not be supposed to be a man who sought safety by submitting to what custom has taught others to consider as a disgrace.

The duel between Aaron Burr, the incumbent US Vice-President, and Alexander Hamilton, former Secretary of the US Treasury, in 1804. Hamilton was mortally wounded and Burr's political career destroyed.

The duel in the rain between Frenchmen Sainte-Beuve and Dubois, the former being a critic and the latter a newspaper editor. Sainte-Beuve insisted on holding his umbrella open while firing his pistol, saying, 'I am quite prepared to be killed, but I do not wish to catch a cold.' Both were unharmed.

I am not presuming to urge anything against the law of God or of this land . . . but upon putting a construction upon my motives, so as to ascertain the quality of my actions, you will make allowance for my situation. It is impossible to define in terms the proper feelings of a gentleman; but their existence has supported this country for many ages, and she might perish if they were lost.

The jury were suitably impressed by Captain Macnamara, whose excellent character was endorsed by Lord Nelson himself, and he was acquitted.

Napoleon disapproved of duelling but there was little he could do to stop it, so entrenched was the practice among his officers. A bill for the suppression of duelling was presented in the Conseil d'Etat, but was rejected after discussion, one of the reasons being:

There is a multitude of offences which legal justice does not punish, and amongst these offences there are some so indefinable, or concerned with matters so delicate, that the injured party would blush to bring them out into broad daylight in order to demand public justice. In these circumstances it is impossible for a man to right himself otherwise than by a duel.

The new nation of the United States lost a number of favourite sons to the iniquitous custom imported from the Old World. In July 1804, Alexander Hamilton, founder of the Bank of New York and former Secretary of the US Treasury, was mortally wounded in a duel with Aaron Burr, then the incumbent Vice-President to Thomas Jefferson. Their fatal meeting was the culmination of many years of political rivalry and enmity. It would appear that Burr was the more vindictive and pressed for the duel, claiming that Hamilton had insulted him. Hamilton was opposed to duelling, his son having been killed in that manner, but with great reluctance he accepted the challenge.

The duel took place at Weehawken Heights, New Jersey, a popular duelling ground just above the Hudson, the same place where Hamilton's son had fallen two years before. They fired their Wogdon pistols at ten paces' distance. Hamilton's shot went wide, deliberately or in error is not sure, but Burr's hit his adversary's liver and caused his death thirty-six hours later. He was forty-seven years old. Hamilton had been a popular figure and his wasteful death generated sorrow and indignation throughout the Northern States and gave rise to an anti-duelling movement. Burr's honour may have been satisfied but his killing of Hamilton ruined his life. Charged with murder in New Jersey and driven from New York, he fled south to Georgia and Virginia where duelling was viewed with tolerance. He died in poverty in 1836.

The last recorded duel in England, between Englishmen in the traditional manner, took place in 1845, on the coast near Portsmouth, and involved First Lieutenant Henry Hawkey of the Royal Marines and James Seton, late of the 11th Hussars. Seton had paid too much attention to Hawkey's wife and at a party the marine exploded with the challenge: 'Seton, you're a blackguard and a villain! You can either fight me or be horsewhipped down the Portsmouth High Street.' They agreed to a pistol duel the next day. Both were dressed in black and fired at fifteen paces. Seton fell badly wounded. Hawkey left the scene in great haste, saying, 'I'm off to France.' Seton was carried by boat to the Quebec Hotel, on the water's edge at Portsmouth, where he died ten days later. Hawkey disappeared; he was dismissed the service in his absence, and nothing more was recorded of him.

Serious duelling remained *de rigueur* in France, as it did in the Southern States of America, till the twentieth century. Today, duelling pistols made by master gunsmiths are beautiful pieces of craftsmanship cloaked in dark history, and fine examples command very high prices when offered for sale.

4
SINGLE SHOT
AND MAGAZINE

General Colbert raised his sabre. At his signal, the French chasseurs and hussars launched themselves against the stubborn British rearguard guarding the bridge over the Cua at Cacabelos. In the fearful January weather of 1809, Sir John Moore's almost broken army was in retreat to Corunna. Discipline among some of the formations of the rearguard at Cacabelos was breaking. Colbert and the French cavalry rushing upon the British soldiery thought that they had an easy victory over the British rearguard.

But one battalion of the 95th Regiment had been detached to the rearguard. Their discipline was not in doubt. As the French charged, they formed up as best they could to present a front to the horsemen and a wall of fire. They loaded carefully but rapidly, and the first volley tore into the galloping horses. The accurate fire of the green-jacketed riflemen checked

the onrushing horsemen and forced them to retire in confusion. 'We popped them off whenever they showed their ugly faces, like mice in the sun!' said one rifleman.

The riflemen were then ordered to quit their untenable position and join the main column. As they were doing so, Colbert rallied his men and led them in another spirited charge against the enemy.

It was a critical moment for the 95th. They were caught off balance, and into the breach plunged Rifleman Tom Plunkett. He was a noted marksman. He ran into the open, and threw himself flat on the ground. Taking up a sharpshooting position – the sling of his Baker rifle caught over his foot – he took careful aim and shot dead the gallant Colbert. Plunkett jumped to his feet and expertly reloaded his rifle.

The general's orderly-trumpeter had seen the man who had killed his general and dashed straight at the rifleman. Plunkett fired again. The man dropped. Plunkett doubled back to rejoin his comrades. Plunkett had not only taken the heart out of the French charge, but had given the small British force at Cacabelos a victory that stiffened their morale and restored discipline. The British retreat towards the decisive battleground at Corunna continued in a mood of triumph.

THE BAKER RIFLE

The Baker rifle, designed by London gunmaker Ezekiel Baker, was a great advance in accuracy and range over the venerable 'Brown Bess' type of smooth-bore musket, then the standard arm of the British Army. It had a smaller bore than the musket, and its shorter, rifled barrel had seven grooves making a quarter turn along its length. It was sighted for 100 and 200yd. Like the musket, it was loaded at the muzzle and fired by flintlock; the tight-fitting ball had to be rammed down the rifled barrel with ramrod and mallet. The Baker served the rifle regiments for forty years until superseded by the percussion-fired Brunswick rifle.

Other European armies had adopted rifles for certain units before the British decided in 1800 to raise a special regiment, the 95th Foot, armed with the best weapon available. The green-uniformed riflemen soon won a fine reputation in the Napoleonic campaigns. In 1816, after Waterloo, in which battle skirmishers of the 95th claimed to have fired the opening shot, the regiment was honoured by being taken out of the line and given the title of the Rifle Brigade. At the same time, the 60th Foot was converted to a Rifle Regiment.

In *Recollections of Rifleman Harris of the Old 95th*, Harris recalls a sharp-shooting exploit during the Walcheren expedition of 1809:

> I remember a fellow named Jackman getting close up to the walls of Flushing, and working a hole in the earth with his sword, into which he laid himself and remained there alone, despite all efforts of the enemy to dislodge him. He was known, thus earthed, to have killed with the utmost coolness and deliberation eleven French artillerymen as they worked at their guns. As fast

Tom Plunkett shoots General Colbert with his Baker rifle during the retreat to Corunna in 1809.
(Illustration by Harry Payne)

as they relieved each fallen comrade did Jackman pick them off; after which he took to his heels and got safe back to his comrades.

RIFLING AND PERCUSSION IGNITION

Rifling – from the German *riffeln*, to groove – was introduced to gunmaking in sixteenth-century Vienna and Nuremberg, the first patent for rifling being granted to Arnold Rotsipen in 1635. Rifling consists of spiral grooves cut into the bore of the barrel. The grooves impart a spin to the ball or bullet as it leaves the muzzle. This spinning keeps the projectile in an accurate line towards the target. The whole force of the charge was utilised in propelling the ball because it fitted so tightly in the rifled bore that the gases, caused by the explosion of the charge, could not escape around it.

Muzzle-loaded rifles were even slower to load than the smooth-bore musket, for it required time and strength to ram home the tight-fitting ball. Therefore, rifle-making flourished in countries where hunting game and target shooting were popular, such as the forest lands of north and central Europe and colonial North America, where accuracy and range were more important than rapid fire. German and Swiss emigrants to the New World transplanted their rifle-making skills. The rebel colonists in the American War of Independence used their long 'Kentucky' rifles with telling effect against the British redcoats armed with the 'Brown Bess' musket.

A great stride forward in the development of firearms came with the introduction of percussion ignition, which replaced the flintlock. It was invented by the Scotsman Alexander Forsyth who, after many years of trials and experiments, produced a lock which he patented in 1807. 'The Forsyth patent gun-lock,' he claimed, 'is entirely different from the common gun-lock. It produces inflammation by means of percussion, and supersedes the use of flints.' His principle was to employ a small amount of detonating powder which, when struck by the gun hammer, flashed through the touch-hole and ignited the powder in the barrel. The percussion cap, a development of Forsyth's system and a great improvement, came into use about 1820. As with most technological innovations, the military were slow to adopt the percussion system, but its utter superiority over the flintlock led the British in 1836 to arm the 2nd Battalion, The Rifle Brigade, with the new Brunswick percussion rifle.

Means of ignition had improved, but the problem remained of loading a ball down the rifle barrel without the necessity of ramming and hammering. This was necessary because the ball had to fit tightly to seal the bore and – in rifles – grip the rifling. Several types of ammunition were devised to overcome this. In 1847, Captain Minié of the French Army produced a successful bullet, cylindro-conoidal in

RIFLES AT WATERLOO

An eyewitness account by Captain W. Eeles of the Battle of Waterloo gives dramatic insight into the power of the rifle on the field of battle and into the value of formations. It gives some idea of what the average rifleman suffered, with stoic discipline, in obedience to his superior's orders. It is noteworthy also for his observations about cavalry against infantry. At Waterloo, the French cavalry were mercilessly squandered in charge upon charge at the British line: swept with cannon fire as they advanced, cut down by volley after volley of rifle fire as they approached the line, and then chased back with cannon fire as they retreated, the dead, dying and wounded cavalry fell in their hundreds. They continued to charge until their horses were too exhausted to advance at more than a trot. They were vanquished by the rifle and the cannon.

Eeles commanded one of the two companies of the 3rd Battalion of the 95th Rifles, which, together with the 52nd and 71st Regiments and the 2nd Battalion 95th Rifles formed General Adams' 3rd British Brigade of Infantry at Waterloo. The Brigade lost many of its men as they faced the firepower of French artillery. In the early afternoon, the Brigade advanced onto the field, under cover of smoke from a heavy exchange of artillery between the British and French batteries.

. . . on the smoke clearing away, the 71st Regiment, with whom my company of the 3rd Battalion 95th Regiment was then acting, found itself while in column very close to and in front of a large body of the Enemy's Infantry, formed in lines, and dressed in grey coats. The 71st immediately formed line, and I placed my Company of Rifles on the right of that Regiment . . . the French and 71st were closer than I ever before saw any regular formed adverse bodies, and much nearer than troops usually engage. The French opened a very heavy fire on the 71st, who, nevertheless, completed their formation in the most regular and gallant style. I formed my Company on their right, and in line. During this operation the 71st and the Company of the 95th suffered severely, but immediately on being formed succeeded in repulsing the Enemy, who retired almost unobserved in the smoke. Finding, however, notwithstanding the retreat of the French, that many men, both in the 71st and the Company of the 95th, were still falling, I moved my Company forward, and found a considerable number of the Enemy in a dell in a rye field, from which place they were firing on the 71st.

The Company I commanded immediately attacked and drove them back to their position on the hill. While we were so employed I observed a large body of the Enemy's Cavalry advancing to attack us. We had just time to get back and form in rear of the 71st Square, when the Enemy attacked that Regiment with much impetuosity and determination.

The charge was received with the utmost coolness and gallantry by the 71st.

The Cavalry were repulsed in this instance, and in all their other attacks, without occasioning the least loss or disorder to the Square of the 71st. During one of these charges of the Enemy's Cuirassiers on the right angle of the front face of the 71st Square, I moved my Company from the rear to the right, in line with the rear face of the Square, and placing myself in front of it, kept every man from firing until the Cuirassiers approached within thirty or forty yards of the Square, when I fired a volley from my Company which had the effect, added to the fire of the 71st, of bringing so many horses and men at the same moment to the ground, that it became quite impossible for the Enemy to continue their charge . . .

I mention this merely to prove how perfectly impossible it is for Cavalry to arrive in sufficient force against Infantry, so as to be at all dangerous, if the Infantry will only be steady, and give their fire all at once.

After these various attacks of Cavalry had failed, everything remained for some time in a state of comparative quiet, and the Brigade remained in squares . . .

As the Regiments of the 3rd Brigade were found to suffer from the Enemy's shot, while so exposed in the hollow, they moved back to the crest of the hill about six o'clock . . . During this time the Enemy was forming his Infantry for the last attack . . . the 'Crisis of the Battle'. To meet this attack the 3rd Brigade was formed in line four deep . . .

The brigade when so formed were on a height, or rather a little behind it, being brought considerably forward from the British line, so as to be able to bring their full front on the flank of the French advancing to the attack . . . after a violent cannonade from the British Guns, the 3rd Brigade opened a heavy fire and advanced on the line in which they had been placed.

The 3rd Battalion 95th regiment moved on at the same time, and very shortly, as the 52nd and 71st opened out a little, was formed in line between these two Regiments. When the smoke cleared away a little I found that we were moving between both Armies and driving some French before us in the greatest disorder.

British squares stand firm against mass French cavalry attacks. (Scene from the 1970 film Waterloo*, courtesy of Columbia Pictures Industries Inc.)*

I was almost immediately ordered out to skirmish with my Company, and continued advancing in that manner until some English and German Dragoons, followed by some French, passed along the front of the Brigade. At the noise of the advancing horsemen, the Company of the 3rd Battalion, which was in front, ran in on the other Company, which was still between the 52nd and 71st. From that time it continued so to advance in that close and compact order, until the Brigade, still formed in line and four deep, came up to three Columns of the Old Imperial Guard, which they attacked and defeated . . .

The Companies of the 3rd Battalion 95th were then again extended, and followed the retiring French, until they came near . . . the farm of Rossomme. I . . . checked the advance of the Riflemen . . . There was, however, no Enemy to attack.

Gurkhas of the British Army armed with the Snider-Enfield of 1867, the first standard issue breech-loader used by British troops. (Painting by Richard Simkin)

shape with a hollow base, which expanded to seal the bore on firing. Rifles and ammunition of the Minié type were adopted by most military powers and saw service with the British in the Crimean War of 1854–6 and in the American Civil War of 1861–5.

The Minié was relatively easy to load. The soldier bit open the paper cartridge, poured the powder down the barrel, rammed in the paper to seat the charge, then rammed the bullet home. He then placed the percussion cap over the nipple, full cocked the hammer, aimed and fired. When fired, the force of the explosion expanded the hollow base of the cylindro-conoidal bullet to fit the rifling tightly, thus sealing the bore and giving the bullet a sure grip on the rifling. The projectile left the barrel spinning, with considerable accuracy and sustained velocity.

The effective range of the Minié-type rifle was about 400 to 600yd compared with 100 to 200yd for smooth-bore muskets. The rate of fire was theoretically 3 rounds per minute, but this was seldom attained either in practice or in battle.

The Martini-Henry in action with British redcoats in Afghanistan, 1880. (Illustration by W. O. Overend)

Constant firing caused fouling in the barrel and repeated jamming, so soldiers were issued with 'Williams bullets' for use after every ten shots: these special slugs had a thin metal disc that was supposed to clean out the barrel on discharge.

BOLT-ACTION BREECH LOADING

The next significant progression in military rifles was the introduction of bolt-action breech loading. Prussia pioneered the way in 1848 with the 'needle gun' designed by Nicholas von Dreyse. This rifle had a bolt, held in position by a projection fitting into a notch. The bolt had a knob which was turned upwards and drawn back, thus leaving the breech open for loading. The needle, or striker, was held back in withdrawing the bolt; on pressing the trigger, the needle flew forward and pierced the cartridge, detonating the explosive charge. Cartridges were of the self-consuming type, made of material that burned away in the chamber on the explosion of the charge.

This rifle was adopted as standard Prussian in 1842 and was the general arm of the victorious Prussian and German troops in the wars of 1848, 1866 and 1870. In the Austro-Prussian War of 1866, the technical superiority of the needle gun over the Austrian muzzle-loader undoubtedly shortened the battle to only seven weeks in duration.

The Dreyse rifle had its faults – for example, the long needle quickly corroded and broke and the escape of gas at the breech made it frightening to fire – yet the gain in rapidity of loading, in all positions, far outweighed its defects. Prussian soldiers were trained to fire 5 rounds a minute, a big advance on the rate of fire of muzzle-loaders. Maximum range was about 800yd. Each soldier carried sixty rounds – and a spare needle.

Wilhelm I is attributed with saying:

> A three-hundred-men detachment of Prussians is the equal in firepower to nine hundred enemy soldiers and is less vulnerable because the three hundred men present but one third of the frontal length of the enemy battalion.

The French adopted the Chassepot-system needle gun in 1866, using a combustible cartridge similar to that used by the Prussian Dreyse. Sweden, Russia and Italy all embraced bolt-action breech-loading rifles in the 1860s. The first breech-loader to be issued to British troops was the Snider-Enfield of 1867, an expedient conversion of the standard Enfield rifled musket. The new weapon did not use the needle principle; it had a block breech action designed by Jacob Snider, a Dutch-American. The trigger operated an external hammer that struck a pin fitted into the breech-block which, in turn, hit the percussion cap to detonate the charge.

French infantry ot the line, 1888, equipped with the new Lebel rifle.

INTERIM RIFLES

The Snider-Enfield, though serviceable, was a stop-gap until the arrival of the Martini-Henry in 1871. This rifle had a falling-block breech mechanism devised by the Austrian Frederic von Martini and a rifled barrel with seven grooves designed by the Edinburgh gunsmith Alexander Henry (no relation of his American contemporary, Tyler Henry). The breech was opened by depressing a large lever behind the trigger guard, which also extracted and ejected the empty case and cocked the rifle. The cartridge, containing bullet, powder and means of ignition, was devised by Colonel Boxer and had an all-metal case of coiled brass with the percussion cap in the centre of the base. Kipling refers to the rifle in his barrack-room ballad 'The Young British Soldier':

> When 'arf of your bullets fly wide in the ditch,
> Don't call your Martini a cross-eyed old bitch;
> She's human as you are – you treat her as sich,
> An' she'll fight for the young British soldier . . .

In the United States, following the Civil War, the Ordnance Department decided to convert fifty thousand muzzle-loading rifle-muskets into breech-loaders using the system engineered by E. S. Allin of the Springfield US Armoury. The Allin system

The bolt-action breech-loaded Dreyse 'needle gun,' Model 1862. The original Dreyse revolutionised rifle design.

incorporated a hinged breech-block that could be raised, like a trap door, to expose the chamber and eject the spent cartridge; a fresh cartridge was then inserted by hand into the chamber, the breech-block was pushed down and the side hammer cocked for firing.

The Allin conversion served the US Army from 1864 until the adoption of the so-called 'trapdoor' Springfield Model of 1873. After testing more than one hundred types of rifle, the Ordnance Board settled for the tried and tested Springfield Allin system. The Model 1873 was a sturdy, reliable weapon with a simple mechanism, long range and excellent stopping power, firing a .45in (11.43mm)

Corporal Long of the 17th Lancers takes aim with his Martini-Henry breech-loaded carbine during skirmishing drill in 1896.

calibre bullet. With certain improvements, the trap-door Springfield served with the regular army until 1892, when the Krag-Jorgensen bolt-action magazine rifle was put into service.

SMALL BORE

France started a trend for military rifles of a smaller calibre by adopting in 1886 the Lebel bolt-action rifle in 8mm (.314in) calibre, to replace the 11mm (.43in) Gras rifle of 1874. Named after Colonel Nicholas Lebel of the Military Commission, the rifle held nine rounds in a tubular magazine under the barrel (similar to the US Winchester repeater). The Lebel used the first successful high-pressure smokeless cartridge containing the secret powder known as Poudre B (after War Minister Marshal Boulanger). Stringent precautions were taken to keep secret the composition of the charge; it was forbidden to open cartridges on penalty of ten years' imprisonment. But the secret got out and Germany and other nations began experimenting

with smokeless cartridges which, compared with cartridges using black powder, gave off little or no gunsmoke.

Germany had replaced the needle gun in 1871 with the rifle designed by Paul Mauser to fire metal cartridges. The success of the bolt-action Mauser, and its improved models, led to its being taken into service by the armies of many nations which did not have their own arms industry. Mauser Models 1893/5 contained virtually all the design features that made the German rifle universally popular including the front locking lugs that gave great strength to the action, and the five-shot clip that was swiftly and easily loaded into the top of the magazine section and held in a fixed box within the stock. Using a smokeless cartridge, the Mauser's 7mm (.276in) calibre bullet had a flat trajectory, producing low recoil and a high degree of accuracy.

When the Boer Republics of South Africa declared war on Great Britain in October 1899, the crackshot Boer farmers, organised into horse-mounted commando units, were well armed with the Mauser Model 1895, of which fifty thousand had been purchased from Germany before hostilities broke out. The British, armed with the Lee-Enfield, came to respect the Mauser and the Boer marksmen, who usually fired or sniped from long distance, from a concealed position. The Mauser Model 1898, and the Mauser turnbolt-action Kar 98k in 7.92mm (.312in) calibre, served the German Army in both world wars; the 'kar' is short for karabiner, or carbine. Made under licence in many countries, the Kar 98k is still in service in parts of the world.

The British Army's Martini-Henry single-shot was replaced in 1888 by the Lee-Metford bolt-action, eight-round magazine rifle in .303in (7.7mm) calibre; the Mark Two conversion had a ten-round magazine

capacity. This new weapon married the bolt-action breech and detachable magazine produced by Scotsman James P. Lee and the seven-grooved rifled barrel designed by Englishman William E. Metford. It fired a solid-drawn brass cartridge; the powder was smokeless cordite. The cordite, however, caused erosion to the Metford rifling and led to the adoption of a five-groove system, developed at the government factory at Enfield, resulting in the Lee-Enfield rifle of 1896.

SMLE AND THE BEF

For the British Army's rifleman, the Third Boer War had two important consequences. First, experience with the Lee-Enfield rifle in the war led to a shortened version, designated the Short Magazine Lee-Enfield, or SMLE. This weapon served as the standard rifle of the British Army and Empire forces in both world wars, and into the 1950s, when it was finally replaced by the Self Loading Rifle (SLR) of Belgian origin. Secondly, during the Third Boer War, the shooting ability of the British infantry had been found wanting. After the war, a policy of exacting training in marksmanship and rapid fire was implemented.

Despite the low standard of rifle work, the British government refused to accept the necessity of equipping the army with machine guns. To improve marksmanship, and to overcome the lack of machine gun firepower, Lt-Colonel McMahon, Chief Instructor at the School of Musketry at Hythe, introduced a new rifle training programme in 1909. The result was that by 1914 men of the regular infantry could fire 15 rounds a minute with accuracy, and many could fire

'The Skirmish Line,' from a painting by Charles Schreyvogel, showing the Indian-fighting US Cavalry of the 1870s armed with the single-shot Springfield carbine Model 1873.

(above) *Boer commandos armed with the excellent Mauser Model 1895. The Boers purchased fifty thousand of these rifles just before the war with the British.*

(below) *British cavalry pursuing the Boers after the relief of Kimberley in 1900. The cavalry carried Lee-Metford and Lee-Enfield carbines.* (From a painting by the American artist Frederic Remington)

20 rounds a minute with high scores – a rate unequalled by any army.

When the regulars of the small but highly efficient British Expeditionary Force (BEF) landed in France soon after the start of World War One, they were without doubt the finest disciplined riflemen in the world. It was the BEF, commanded by Sir John French, who bore the full brunt of the first, concentrated German attacks.

At Mons in August 1914, the rapid fire of the British ten-shot magazine SMLE decimated the massed ranks of the advancing Germans. The rapid bolt-action fire of the British stunned and stopped the grey German hordes from steamrollering over France. So fast and devastating was the rifle fire that the Germans were under the impression that the BEF was equipped with hundreds of machine guns. The Germans advanced en masse in close order and 'were simply blasted away to Heaven at seven hundred yards', commented a member of the BEF, 'and in their insane formation every bullet was almost sure to find two billets.'

The German Army was brought to a halt and von Kluck, the commander, had to change his original plan. 'After we had broken through the French positions,' reported a member of the German General Staff on the battle of Mons, 'the advance was checked . . . the Englishman shoots magnificently, extraordinarily well.' On 24 August, the hail of rapid fire produced by a single battalion of the Duke of Wellington's Regiment drove back six enemy battalions.

The BEF was virtually wiped out but it conducted the masterly retreat from Mons, and, in September 1914, the BEF finally turned at the Marne to inflict a decisive defeat on the enemy. The German hopes of

'How the Mauser Rifle is Loaded' published in the British magazine The Illustrated War News of 23 December 1914.

a speedy victory were destroyed: 'I always had the greatest admiration for the BEF,' von Kluck wrote. 'It was the wonderful kernel of a great army. The way the retreat was carried out was remarkable.'

Although the Germans slowed down and advanced with caution, it was at the sacrifice of the BEF – there were no equally as well-trained replacements to compensate for the BEF's heavy casualties. They were the last of a bolt-action breed – never again could the British Army field such superb single-shot riflemen. Such magnificent riflemen could not be replaced by wartime volunteers and conscripts.

THE BAYONET

On the field of Corunna on 16 January 1809, the Black Watch fell back, owing to a misunderstanding of orders, to replenish their ammunition. Lt-General

LUCKY CORPORAL LAURI

There are many well-documented examples of soldiers in battle who escape death from bullets in the most amazing manner. Bullets have been deflected or stopped on their fatal flight by all kinds of items carried by soldiers: cigarette tins, pipes, 'eating irons', coins, keys, and the most appropriate of life-saving obstructions – the Bible. Private Perkins of the British 1st Lincolnshire Regiment had a Bible in his left breast pocket when he was hit by a German bullet in France, in 1915. The missile, according to a contemporary report, 'passed through a number of pages then glanced off with its deadly mission unfulfilled.'

In surviving bullets in battle Corporal Lauri of the Seaforth Highlanders was incredibly fortunate. As he charged a Dervish barrier at Atbara in the Sudan, on 8 April 1898, a bullet ripped off the toe of his left boot without touching his foot. Another bullet struck his bayonet and bent it at right angles. A third slug tore a hole in his left sleeve. As he reloaded his Lee-Enfield magazine rifle, a bullet splintered the butt and ricocheted off the steel bolt, buzzing bee-like past his head.

Moments later, a huge Dervish sprang at Lauri, jabbing with a spear that did not harm the Scotsman but ripped open his haversack. Yet another bullet seared his knuckles, drawing blood. Finally, as the fight drew to a close, an enemy rifleman fired almost vertically up at him. This bullet penetrated his right-hand ammunition pouch and tunic pocket, smashing a penknife and two pencils, and inflicting only a slight surface wound across his chest. Corporal Lauri was lucky indeed that day.

A CLEAN KILL

The notice on the entrance to the sniper's post was peremptory, personal and clear:

**SNIPERS POST No 1
OUT OF BOUNDS TO ALL TROOPS
EXCEPT SNIPER ON DUTY
KEEP OUT!
THIS MEANS *YOU*!**

The curtain was drawn across the entrance. The sniper on duty was a young Royal Scot from Leith, Private Sandy Burns. This morning, in the clarity after the summer dawn, he was looking very hard across the desolation of No Man's Land. He had a target in mind.

The sniper's post was fairly new. It had been carefully sited to coordinate with the other posts in the sector and cover the German front and support lines to maximum ability. The field of view from the post was limited, but the areas of each post overlapped, covering all the ground laterally with the capacity for enfilade fire. The distance to the German line was not too great, not too short and visibility was unobstructed. Burns' target was in view.

From a prefabricated structure, the post had been built at night and was carefully camouflaged. Every night, the duty sniper inspected the post from No Man's Land, to ensure it was invisible. The Germans were still unaware it was there. Had they been, it would have been trench-mortared out of existence. The Germans might shortly want to find the post very badly.

Private Burns checked his rifle and sight. The rifle, an Enfield 1914, Snipers Pattern, with five-round magazine, was used only as a sniper. The type had been introduced only weeks before in April 1918, officially designated the Mark 1*W(T). Only three rifles of this pattern had been allotted to each battalion. It was a fine rifle, but not to be given to the 'brutal and licentious' soldiers who might be tempted to fix a bayonet on it for bloody and vicious bayonet work as this would wreck the accuracy. This was a precision instrument for assassination.

It would never be used by anyone else, for if the rifle were used by different men, best results could not be obtained. Nor would it be worn out by practice shooting. After eight hundred rounds had been fired through the barrel, the extreme accuracy would begin to fall off as a result of erosion and other factors. All other shooting would be carried out with an ordinary open-sighted rifle. Burns' telescopic-sighted rifle would be used only for either zeroing or, as he put it, 'killing Huns'. This morning, he was going to kill a colonel.

He was an excellent shot, one of the best, otherwise he would never have been given this job – a telescopic sight can never make a bad shot into a good one. The chief value of a telescopic sight is that it gives a clearer, enlarged definition of the target, so allowing a definite aim to be laid on the exact spot the sniper wished to hit. Burns had the spot he wanted to hit already decided, but he would not have much time.

That was the second advantage of the telescopic sight – it allowed quicker aiming and firing. There were only two things to align – the pointer and the target mark, and these were already in focus. On an open-sighted rifle, there were three things to align – backsight, foresight and mark. Burns needed this grace. He would have only a few seconds in which to fire and hit.

The young Royal Scot adjusted his position on his mat. He cupped the rifle in his left hand, and settled his elbow. He brought the rifle butt into his right shoulder. The wood of the butt was solid, and heavy, against his cheek. He could smell cordite, and a hint of gun oil – he always tried to use as little gun oil as possible, it gave off smoke when the gun was fired and would increase the risk of his being spotted. He tucked his right finger around the trigger, gently – the Enfield Sniper was very easy to pull off compared to the SMLE.

He checked that the eyepiece was perfectly clear and luminous, without any ring or shadow. Burns was using an Aldis No 4 sight. For practical purposes, a magnification of 2½ to 4

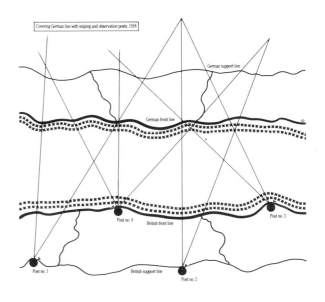

Covering German line with sniping and observation posts, 1918

German support line

German front line

British front line

Post no. 4

Post no. 3

Post no. 1

British support line

Post no. 2

was sufficient – if it was too powerful, the glass would magnify errors.

The sniper had the sight's focus already adjusted to show a clearly defined image. He had it zeroed – the scope and the man would be in unison, with every chance of hitting a small mark. A sniper's maximum range was about 600yd, so the maximum effect was got by arranging the line of sight and the line of fire to cross about midway. All scopes were calibrated to hit the point aimed at, so a 6 o'clock aim was not taken – as with an open-sighted rifle – but aim was laid on the exact spot to be hit.

A bullet will fall during its flight – the rifle's muzzle should, then, be raised above the point one wishes to hit. Burns expertly calculated the elevation that he would require. The rule was simple, learnt by heart at the First Army School, Glencorse: 'Multiply range figure by next higher and the result will give number of inches higher for 100yd increase in range . . .' He checked the

slight hill above the British front line, a perfect opportunity to kill him.

Burns watched. The orderly's head came into view. Burns' breathing slowed. His finger rested lightly on the trigger – careful not to fire too soon. The orderly had the towel out. The sniper began to count – 'one, two, three . . .' the colonel's head appeared . . . 'five . . .' The Enfield crashed. The butt slammed into the sniper's shoulder. He kept his eye on the scope eyepiece. The bullet, travelling at 2,700 feet (823m) per second, hit the colonel in the back of the head as he wound the towel around his torso. There was a spray of something – or was it the sniper's imagination? The orderly stood rigid, with blood and bits of cranium covering his face. The colonel had disappeared.

The sniper had a milli-second to decide not to kill the orderly too and moved back from the loophole, just in case his shot had been observed by an enemy sniper. He laid the gun

Zeroing snipers' rifles fitted with telescopic sights

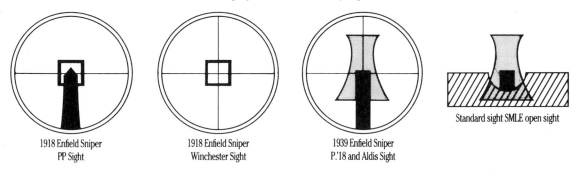

| 1918 Enfield Sniper PP Sight | 1918 Enfield Sniper Winchester Sight | 1939 Enfield Sniper P.'18 and Aldis Sight | Standard sight SMLE open sight |

elevation. Then, placing his eye just far enough behind the scope to avoid injury to his eyebrow through the shock of discharge, the sniper laid his aim. It was nearly time.

He noted with quiet satisfaction that the sight was absolutely correct. The line giving the range at which he was firing coincided with the line he was firing at. His heart was beating hard, the rifle jumping slightly. He relaxed, and steadied the rifle. He could smell the gun oil now, and the mud and staleness of the trenches through the loophole plates. But his attention was entirely focussed beyond No Man's Land.

The colonel would be finishing his bath now. He would soon stand up. His orderly would hold the towel stretched out for the colonel to wrap himself around in. For a second or so, the colonel's head would be in full view along a slice out of the ground. That was all it took. The colonel, idiot though he must be for bathing just behind the front line, thought himself secure enough. He could not have seen how the nick out of the land gave a sniper, positioned on a

down carefully, and began to check the magazine, stripping the bolt back, trying not to think about anything.

He would not make a notch on his butt for the man he had killed. He knew that the woodwork of the rifle should never be cut as the inaccuracy which might result could cause the loss of his *own* life.

The 42nd Royal Highlanders, Black Watch, repulse the charge of French Cuirassiers during the Waterloo campaign. (Painting by Harry Payne)

The controlled bayonet charge in modern warfare has been relegated to the annals of heroism. The last British charge was made by the Seaforth Highlanders in 1944. The need to use the bayonet may arise very suddenly. In using bayonets with Lee-Enfield rifles, the British soldier would carry the rifle in the most convenient position, according to the country being traversed, so that he could come on guard quickly, by taking a full pace forward with the left foot and, at the same time, bring the rifle up to a natural fighting position. Fitting the bayonet did not preclude firing the rifle, although it would affect the aim. During an advance and at about 10yd from the enemy, it might be advisable to fire a bullet to deliver an effective blow before getting close enough to kill with the bayonet.

GRENADE LAUNCHERS

Grenades have long been part of an infantryman's armoury. They are useful for a variety of purposes. It was discovered that their effect could be enhanced if they were fired from a rifle-mounted grenade discharger, standard pieces of kit developed by various nations for their infantry rifles. The following grenades relate to the British Rifle No1 and No3.

The No36 grenade was useful for a variety of anti-personnel purposes – clearing dug-outs and buildings, or killing crews of AFVs. It was also useful for any form of close-quarter fighting – wood or street fighting, ambushes, and night fighting. The No36 had the oval cast-iron body with the curved striker lever, held in place by a split pin. The grenade was fairly heavy, and could be thrown from 25–35yd. For further distances, a discharger was used.

The No68 grenade was for anti-AFV purposes and was fired from the rifle discharger. The effective range was from 50–75yd; a rifle-mounted grenade sight was designed for use between these distances. Excellent effect could be obtained against AFVs by allowing them to pass through and engaging them in the rear, where the armour was thinner. The grenade could be fired from the hip, if necessary, against houses. The No68 grenade weighed 1¾lb. The body was filled with HE and closed at front end by a brass disc held in position by a screw-on ring. It was painted buff. The tail unit had vanes to keep it steady during flight. The striker was held in position by a safety pin to which a label was attached, and by a shear wire.

The British Army No1 and No2 grenade dischargers were developed for firing both the Nos68 and 36 grenades from the standard service No1 rifle (SMLE), the No3 rifle (patt. '14) or the .30in (patt. '17 USA). In order to fire a grenade, the discharger was attached to the rifle, which was then loaded with a ballistite cartridge, and the grenade placed in the discharger. When the ballistite cartridge was fired, the grenade was discharged. In firing grenades, ballistite cartridges only were to be used – never ball ammunition.

Moore, the British commander, saw their move. He rode up to his fellow countrymen. 'My brave 42nd,' he exclaimed, 'if you've fired your ammunition, you've still got your bayonets! . . .'

Until the invention of a successful breech-loading rifle, skirmishers fought with bayonets fixed. Musketeers relied upon the power of successive volleys fired from their defensive boxes. Individuals could not rely upon their muskets for defence, as they could not depend upon individual accuracy or rapid loading to thwart a determined enemy assault. If an enemy broke through, musketeers fixed bayonets or drew swords.

Even in modern mechanised warfare, the bayonet has remained one of the infantryman's primary weapons. Experience has shown that the time almost invariably comes when hand-to-hand fighting develops. This usually occurs when the enemy's foremost positions have been penetrated, or in unexpected encounters with small parties in woods, villages and confined spaces, and at night, or when dealing with airborne troops. For such fighting, the bayonet, in the hands of a skilled and determined fighter, has often been the most efficient weapon.

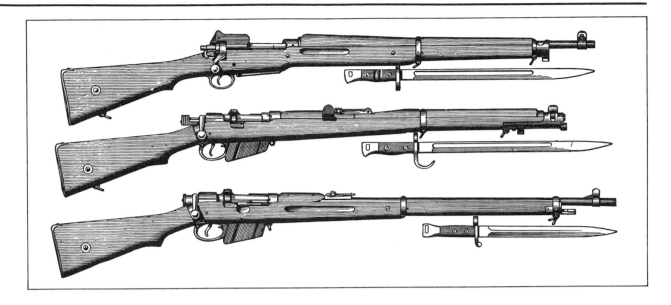

The discharger No1 Mark I was for use with the No1 rifle (SMLE). The barrel was cylindrical and was threaded internally to receive the locking base. Near the lower end was a slot which formed the gas port. This was closed by a sliding shutter, which could be clamped in position by a clamping nut. When firing the No68 grenade, the gas port was kept completely closed. The locking base was threaded on the outside to fit the barrel and had a central hole threaded to receive the adjusting screw, the top of which was slotted to take the point of the bayonet. Below were two claw levers, designed to fit into the slotted sides of the nosecap of the rifle. The barrel of the discharger No2 Mark I was fitted with a ring by means of which the gas was regulated to obtain different ranges.

When using the discharger for the No36 grenade, the rifle was held at an angle of 45 degrees, heel of butt on the ground. The rifleman kept his head well back, his right knee close to his left foot, with his hands (except for the trigger finger) clear of all metal, and the rifle aligned on the target. Ranges, based on the above angle, were obtained by opening or closing the gas port.

To obtain accuracy with the No68 grenade, a sight was designed. The Mark I was used with No1 Rifle. For the No3 and P'17 rifles, the Mark II sight was used. To aim and fire the No68 grenade, the rifleman adopted a position where the rifle could be held at a low angle. The simplest position was lying on the stomach with the left hand holding the rifle in the most convenient position. The head had to be kept well back in order to use the sights. The rifleman aimed quickly through the sights and fired.

ANTI-TANK RIFLES

Anti-tank rifles were developed first by the Germans in World War One to provide forward platoons with immediate protection against the new British tanks.

British Lee-Enfield rifles. Top: *The Pattern 1914, manufactured in the USA and issued to American troops as the Model 1917.* Middle: *The Short Magazine Lee-Enfield (SMLE) used by the British throughout World War One.* Bottom: *The Long Lee-Enfield of 1896.*

British soldier with the Lee-Metford bolt-action magazine rifle that replaced the Martini-Henry in 1888.

Most anti-tank rifles were developed in the 1930s, and could satisfactorily penetrate the armour of a World War One tank, but by 1939, tank armour was thicker. The Polish developed 7.92mm anti-tank rifles; the Germans developed 7.92mm/13mm weapons; the Soviets developed 14.5mm weapons; and the British developed a .55in weapon. None was truly effective against tanks. The 20mm cannons which were then developed were neither mobile platoon weapons, nor practically effective.

The British developed one anti-tank rifle, in the 1930s, which was typical in design and effectiveness. The Rifle, Anti-tank, .55in Boys Mark I and short-barrelled airborne Mark II was designated as a platoon weapon to afford a means of protection against light AFVs. It did have great accuracy, and it was comparatively light and mobile. It did, however, have a pronounced flash and muzzle blast when fired, which was a tactical disadvantage – firing the gun revealed the position and invited retaliation. It also had excessive recoil, although the recoil reducer, strong buffer spring and padded shoulder-piece reduced the effects on the firer. Neither the Mark I nor II entered service. They were superseded by the PIAT.

Although the tungsten-cored bullets developed for anti-tank rifles would – under ideal conditions – penetrate the armour of light AFVs up to 500yd and inflict casualties on the crew, the effective range was well below 300yd. Penetrative power was 10 per cent less at 300yd than at 100yd. The angle of impact of the anti-tank rifle bullet in the armour had a greater influence than the range at which it was fired. Penetrative power was 25 per cent less when the angle of impact was over 20 degrees and 50 per cent less at over 40 degrees at 100yd range. The exact moment of fire would therefore be decided by the firer's determination to hit the selected part of the tank fair and square. As a general rule, an anti-tank rifle bullet could penetrate all parts of the Pz Kw Mk I light tank, and the sides and rear of the hull and turret of the Pz Kw Mk II light tank, at 250yd range at an angle of impact of 20 degrees or less. It would not penetrate the armour of heavier tanks except in certain points such as the rear of the turret and cupola of the Pz Kw Mk IV at very short range.

There were many similarities between the anti-tank rifle and other weapons and soldiers could handle it with a small amount of instruction. The mechanism of an anti-tank rifle was similar to that of a service rifle. Its mode of employment would have been similar to that of an LMG. Anti-tank rifles were not regarded as specialist weapons, and all ranks could be taught to fire them. Men would be trained to aim, at close ranges, at vulnerable parts of tanks and armoured vehicles. In action, the team would consist of two men, one the firer, the other the observer, whose duty it was to observe target in the arc given. In practice, frequently only one man, the firer, would be available. By 1943, it was completely apparent that the infantryman had lost his contest with the tank. He needed more specialised weapons. The use of anti-tank rifles ceased in 1945. Today, the infantryman has at his disposal a range of light, but sophisticated and effective missiles for use against tanks.

Lance-Corporal Michael O'Leary, Irish Guards, won the Victoria Cross in France, February 1915, by storming the enemy position virtually single-handed. Firing his SMLE with coolness and accuracy he killed five Germans at the first barricade, after which he alone attacked and captured a second barricade, taking several prisoners.

PART TWO
THE GOLDEN AGE

It was an August afternoon in 1863. In the Treasury gardens, Washington DC, President Abraham Lincoln lifted the newly developed Spencer repeating rifle to his shoulder, sighted it at the makeshift target forty paces away, and fired. The first bullet hit the board a few inches below the bull's-eye. Lincoln worked the trigger guard lever, a movement which extracted and ejected the spent cartridge and also inserted a fresh shell into the chamber. The president's second shot hit the centre spot. He then swiftly emptied the seven-shot capacity magazine, making a tight grouping very near the bull's-eye.

Pleased with his shooting, Lincoln handed the rifle to one of his companions, Christopher Spencer, saying, 'Now let's see the inventor try his luck.' Spencer reloaded the weapon through an opening in the butt-plate, inserting the metallic rimfire cartridges into the tubular magazine. He fired them in quick succession, besting the president slightly.

Lincoln was much impressed by the weapon and repeated the 'shooting match' the following day, in company with his secretary, John Hay. Lincoln

The Spencer seven-shot repeating carbine.

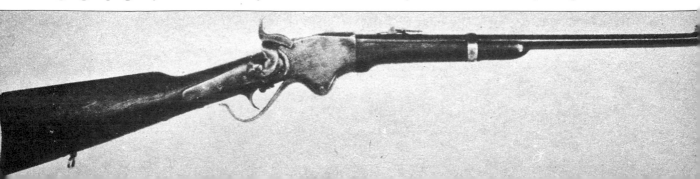

5
MR LINCOLN'S GUN

Percussion lock of the Enfield rifle-musket of 1853.

examined the gun in detail and found to his surprise that it could be field-stripped and reassembled with just a screwdriver. Hay recorded:

> The evening was spent with the president in shooting with Spencer's new repeating rifle, a wonderful gun loading with absolutely contemptible simplicity and ease, with seven balls and firing the whole readily and deliberately in less than half a minute. The president made some pretty good shots. Spencer, the inventor, a quiet little Yankee . . . did some splendid shooting.

With the president's powerful endorsement, the Spencer was put into mass production, in carbine and rifle, to arm the US Army in the great domestic struggle. The Spencer, 'Mr Lincoln's gun,' as it has been called, proved to be the most successful repeater of the Civil War. The US Ordnance Department purchased 94,196 Spencer carbines and 12,471 rifles from 1 January 1861 to 30 January 1866.

Spencer gunfire served the Federal cause very well indeed; but it could have been otherwise save for the timely intervention of Mr Lincoln. Christopher Spencer of Connecticut patented his breech-loading repeater in 1860. It was thoroughly tested by the US Navy and an order was placed. But the new weapon failed to impress or move Brigadier-General Ripley, army chief of Ordnance, a man of conservative if not narrow vision. He distrusted new technology in firearms. He put his faith in the tried and trusted muzzle-loading weapons. The principal infantry weapons of the war were the US Rifle Musket, Model 1861 in .58in (14.8mm) calibre – called the Springfield since it was mostly manufactured at the government arsenal at Springfield, Massachusetts – and the British-made Enfield Rifle Musket, Model 1853, in .577in (14.6mm) calibre.

Ripley regarded the Springfield and the Enfield as excellent weapons. Factories were tooled up and workers trained to produce them efficiently in large

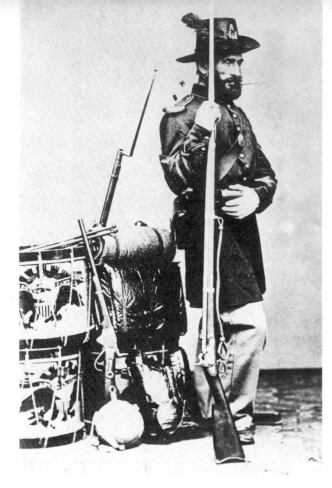

Union soldier holding Minié-type percussion rifle-musket. A Spencer carbine stands against the drum. Note the difference in size of the weapons.

Confederate soldier armed with a British Enfield rifle-musket, a popular weapon with both sides.

numbers, and soldiers were familiarised with these sturdy, simple and reliable firearms which could be topped with a bayonet. Ripley was concerned that the repeating Spencer was too sophisticated, too wasteful of ammunition, perhaps not strong enough to withstand the rigours of infantry service.

In December 1861 Spencer managed to cut through the tangle of red tape and get to Mr Lincoln, who recommended the repeater to Ripley. To be fair to Ripley, when he did place the initial contract for ten thousand Spencer rifles (at $40 each) that same December, the Spencer Repeating Rifle Company of Boston had neither the equipment nor the workforce to fulfil the order. The Spencer company came close to forfeiting this crucial contract. And Ripley was not slow to issue contracts to Samuel Colt's company for revolving pistols.

Soon after the second shooting match with Spencer, in August 1863, Lincoln replaced Ripley with Colonel George D. Ramsey of the Washington arsenal, a man keen on new firearms, and the Spencer went into mass production. In either carbine or rifle version it was used with telling effect in a number of major engagements, in particular by Colonel Wilder's 'Lightning Brigade' of highly mobile mounted infantry.

CIVIL WAR MUZZLE-LOADERS

The Civil War was fought with a profusion of firearms in a great variety of old and new models, some excellent, some indifferent, others downright poor in quality and performance. The outstanding weapons were the Springfield and Enfield rifle muskets, the revolving pistols of Colt and Remington, the Spencer and Henry repeaters, and the Sharps breech-loading single-shot rifle and carbine.

It was Jefferson Davis, Secretary of War in 1853, who directed that infantry be armed with percussion-cap muzzle-loading rifle muskets instead of smooth bore muskets. When civil war broke out, Davis became president of the Confederate States. The technological developments of the nineteenth century had made possible an accurate, dependable muzzle-loading rifle with a rate of fire equal to the smooth-bore musket. This was partly due to the application of the percussion-cap principle to the rifle-lock and partly due to the adoption in 1855 of the French Minié ball. The Civil War was mostly waged with Minié-type rifles, usually called and spelled 'minnie' by soldiers.

When the Civil War broke out, both sides found themselves acutely short of modern firearms. Federal and Confederate agents were sent to Europe to buy

(above) *The Confederate assault on Battery Robinett during the Battle of Corinth.*

(below) *Confederate riflemen in action behind a stone wall during the Battle of Fredericksburg, December 1862.*

(above) *The Battle of Corinth, 1862, a lithograph by Kurz and Allison. Note the regimental flags of the opposing 2nd Texas and the 63rd Ohio.*

(below) *Members of the Southern Skirmish Association re-enact a Civil War battle scene firing black-powder Remington Zouave rifles.*

Captain Schwartz, Union Army, holding a six-shot lever-action Savage revolver, of which more than ten thousand were purchased by the US Ordnance Department.

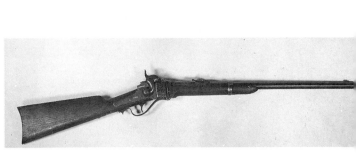

The Sharps breech-loading carbine, a highly regarded weapon widely used by both North and South.

A Sharps rifle with the breech-block, activated by the trigger guard, shown in the lowered position.

what they could. They got a first rate weapon in the British Enfield Rifle Musket, Model 1853, mentioned earlier. About 820,000 of these muzzleloaders were purchased by North and South. The Enfield had a calibre of .577in (14.6mm) and was deadly up to 800yd. It fired a Minié-type bullet. With bayonet fixed, the Enfield had an overall length of 73in and weighed 9.19lb.

The Enfield's US equivalent was the Springfield Model 1861. It had a calibre of .58in and an effective range of 500yd, but could deliver a 'minnie' bullet twice that distance. With bayonet attached it had an overall length of 74in and weighed 9.75lb. Over 670,000 Springfields were manufactured during the Civil War. They cost $19 each.

CIVIL WAR BREECH-LOADERS

There were various types of breech-loading firearms on the market in the 1850s. The US Army began testing all available models but did not complete its tests before 1861. Most Civil War guns were of the percussion type: loaded with lead balls or bullets and black powder and fired by a percussion cap. Effective breech-loading rifles required metallic, as opposed to paper or linen cartridges, in order to prevent gas

escape at the breech. Metallic cartridges were invented in 1856 but were not produced in large numbers until after 1861.

However, the single-shot breech-loading Sharps rifle and carbine, using a paper or linen cartridge, were highly regarded in the Civil War. The US Government purchased ninety thousand of these weapons and over sixteen million Sharps cartridges. The Confederates manufactured copies of the Sharps carbine. The main advantages of the breech-loader over the muzzle-loader were the increased rate of fire (the Sharps, up to 10 rounds a minute) and it could be loaded in the prone position.

The Sharps Rifle

Christian Sharps (1811–74) patented his breech mechanism in 1848. The breech-block, operated by lowering the trigger guard, dropped vertically to expose the chamber for loading the cartridge containing both powder and ball. When the breech-block was closed, by raising it, it sheared off the base of the linen cartridge, thus exposing the powder to the percussion cap flash. It was a sturdy, reliable action. In the 1850s the Sharps rifle won fame in the fighting over the slavery issue in 'Bleeding Kansas'. When anti-slavery preacher Henry Ward Beecher proclaimed that one Sharps rifle contained more moral power 'so far as the slave-holders were concerned than a hundred Bibles,' Sharps rifles became known as 'Beecher's Bibles'. John Brown's followers were armed with Sharps when they made their historic raid on Harper's Ferry.

Two almost identical models of Sharps carbine were manufactured during the Civil War – the .52in calibre New Model 1859 and the New Model 1863. The Sharps rifle Model 1859 was the preferred weapon of the sharpshooter regiments. Colonel Hiram Berdan, a noted marksman, commanded the 1st US Sharpshooters and he insisted on Sharps rifles for his men. In a demonstration before President Lincoln in September 1861, Berdan shot at a man-shaped target called 'Jeff Davis' at 600yd. Lincoln asked Berdan to 'fire at the right eye' – and the crackshot colonel did exactly that! Lincoln gave the order for the desired rifles.

Sharpshooter regiments were usually deployed in small units of snipers and skirmishers to pick off officers and gunners. In the Peninsular Campaign of 1862, a squad of sharpshooters silenced an enemy battery for a considerable time by knocking out the gunners at long range. Berdan's Sharpshooters distinguished themselves at Gettysburg. Berdan handpicked the men, requiring recruits to place ten consecutive shots into a five-inch bull's-eye at 200yd.

'California Joe' Milner, celebrated member of Berdan's 1st US Sharpshooters, photographed after the war when serving as an army scout out West.

Sharpshooters of Berdan's regiment skirmishing in a wheatfield. Colonel Berdan, himself a crackshot, handpicked each of his men for their marksmanship.

The Henry sixteen-shot lever-action repeating rifle, forerunner of the famed Winchester.

Filling cartridges at the US arsenal, Watertown, Massachusetts. Millions of cartridges were consumed in the four years of conflict.

One celebrated member of Berdan's outfit was known only as 'California Joe' (probably Moses Milner who later served as an army scout in the Indian campaigns). A journalist for *Harper's Weekly* penned this contemporary report:

California Joe was first heard of by the public when the army was before Yorktown. I spent an hour yesterday in his tent. He is a character . . . he stands as straight as an arrow, has an eye as keen as a hawk, nerves as steady as can be, and an endowment of hair and whiskers Rubens would have liked for a patriarchal portrait. He has spent years shooting grizzly bears in the forests and fastnesses of California, and carries a telescopic rifle that in his hand will carry a long way and with terrific accuracy. For several days past he has occupied as a shooting place a hole dug in the ground just big enough for himself. His unerring rifle has made many a rebel bite the dust.

The Spencer Rifle

The Spencer repeater was used by the 'Lightning Brigade' of US mounted infantry commanded by Colonel John T. Wilder. On 24 June 1863, Wilder engaged a superior enemy force at Hoover's Gap, Tennessee. The Confederates opened the battle with a spirited infantry charge inspired by the fierce rebel yell. The Southerners expected to pay a heavy toll at the enemy's first volley, but believed that it would take the Union soldiers 45 seconds to recharge their muzzle-loaders. In that time, they would be among them. The Southerners were ignorant of the Spencers that opposed them.

The *Chicago Evening Journal* reported the battle in its 16 July issue:

. . . Five regiments of rebel infantry rose from the low ground near the stream and, cheering like men confident of easy victory, and disposed to inspire terror in their antagonists, came charging across the rolling but open field towards the 17th Indiana [placed by Wilder in the centre position]. The odds were heavily against us, but the boys, armed with the splendid Spencer rifle . . . coolly waited for the auspicious moment.

The enemy approached within easy range, and received a tearing volley from the 17th, that

checked but did not stay them. Supposing our guns exhausted, a cheer followed the report and they moved on. Again the exhaustless weapons pour in their rain of bullets, and still the enemy press on. The rebels were nearing the line in largely superior force and the Colonel looked anxiously for assistance . . .

It seemed that the thin blue line of the 17th Indiana would be overwhelmed by the determined advance. Reinforcements arrived just in time:

Colonel Funkhouser, on a double quick, threw his regiment [the 98th Illinois] on the enemy's flank, and, with the same murderous Spencer rifle, was mowing him at every volley, and moving forward, a perfect avalanche of destruction. The enemy faltered, staggered back, and, as

The Battle of Kennesaw Mountain in 1864, a lithograph published by Kurz and Allison, giving some idea of the heavy black-powder gunsmoke generated in Civil War combat.

if hurried to a decision by the united fire of the 98th and 17th, turned their backs and fled, leaving a large portion of their dead and wounded on the field.

The fight at Hoover's Gap cost the Confederates nearly five hundred dead and wounded, against forty-seven killed in Wilder's Brigade. In this battle, with its first real demonstration of sustained gunfire, the Spencer established its reputation as a death-dealing instrument that could swing the balance of power in a contest of arms.

The Henry Rifle

Another highly regarded repeater of the Civil War was the Henry rifle, the sixteen-shot forerunner of the Winchester, developed by Benjamin Tyler Henry. A young Indiana infantryman wrote of his newly acquired Henry, for which he had paid $35:

They are good shooters and I like to think I have so many shots in reserve . . . I think the Johnnys [enemy] are getting rattled; they are afraid of our repeating rifles. They say we are not fair, that we have guns that load on Sunday and shoot all the rest of the week.

The Henry was manufactured by the New Haven Arms Company of Connecticut, headed by Oliver F. Winchester. A shrewd businessman, he had established himself in firearms manufacture in 1857, when he purchased the assets of the Volcanic Repeating Arms Company, which had produced pistols and rifles featuring a special repeating mechanism actuated by a trigger-guard lever. Winchester organised a new company, the New Haven Arms Company, and made Benjamin Tyler Henry, a brilliant firearms mechanic, the superintendent of the plant. In 1858, Henry devised a self-contained metal-cased rimfire cartridge, holding both the powder and bullet; the base contained a fulminate which, when struck on its edge or rim by the hammer mechanism, fired the charge. He developed the Henry, based on the Volcanic Arms system, to shoot the new ammunition.

The gun was operated by moving the trigger-guard lever down and then back to its original position, a swift, easy action that extracted the spent case, moved a fresh shell from the spring-activated magazine into the chamber, and cocked the hammer ready for firing. The Henry served well in the American Civil War.

About ten thousand Henry repeaters were used in the Civil War, mostly purchased individually by soldiers or by regiments who preferred that particular weapon. Major David C. Gamble, commanding the 66th Illinois Infantry Volunteers, wrote a glowing commendation for the Henry rifle to Oliver Winchester in a letter dated 1 June 1865:

Dear Sir,

I take pleasure in acknowledging the receipt of seven cases of Henry Repeating Rifles . . . It will be gratifying to the New Haven Arms Company to know how highly the Rifle is prized in this command. At no time has the regiment had more than two hundred of these arms in an engagement, yet where other regiments, and even brigades, have given back or failed to press the enemy back, the 66th Illinois, with the assistance of these Rifles, have ever been enabled to hold a position or take one at pleasure . . .

On the morning of 9th May 1864, at Snake Creek Gap, Ga., the 9th Illinois Infantry, armed with the Spencer Rifle, was attacked by Wheeler's brigade of rebel cavalry, and though they fought bravely, and were assisted by the 51st Illinois Infantry, armed with the Springfield rifle musket and bayonet, they were compelled to fall back on the main body of the division, and lost a number of prisoners to the enemy. The 66th Illinois was ordered forward and eight companies deployed as skirmishers; and that line of skirmishers alone, without difficulty, checked the enemy's advance and finally drove him, with much loss, nine miles, to Ressacca, notwithstanding he was reinforced by three regiments of infantry. This affair was witnessed by Generals McPherson, Logan, Dodge, Sweeny and Fuller, and the regiment was highly commended.

Said Gen. G. M. Dodge: 'The idea of a line of skirmishers driving a line of battle, making a charge, and a successful one, and that without

Confederate marksmen picking off defenders of Fort Pillow in April 1864.

bayonets, too, is a new one and a good one, and speaks volumes for the Henry Rifle'. Said he, 'I shall always favor its use in my command.'

Your rifle is light, strong, durable, accurate, quick of firing, easily loaded, safe, and not encumbered with a bayonet, and with a cartridge of a better calibre than the Spencer, and, in my judgement, and to my knowledge, the better arm for the service. I believe, if proper effort was made, it would be introduced into every branch of the army and navy. Armed with the Henry Rifle, with the light accoutrements required for it, infantry can carry 200 cartridges, if necessary, enough for any battle of the war; and, with the advantage of loading and firing, lying down, or in any other position, needs no bayonets, which would only be an encumberance.

WESTERN FIREARMS

The final period of conflict to decide the settlement of the North American West between the white immigrants, supported by the US Army, and the Indians of the Plains came between the end of the Civil War in 1865 and 1890. The Indians fought gallantly and won some battles but the result was never in doubt – the whiteman imposed his civilisation upon the great wilderness. The fiercest resistance came from the Sioux, Cheyenne, Comanche and Kiowas, the Nez Perce of the North-West and Apaches of the South-West.

While the Civil War raged, the Plains Indians took advantage of the situation to raid settlements and trails left unguarded by government troops. Then came the reckoning. The guns and the men who had fought the war headed West to punish and subdue the redman.

Forsyth's Frontiersmen

On 24 August 1868, Brevet-Colonel George A. Forsyth, US Army, was directed by Major-General Philip H. Sheridan to:

> employ fifty first-class hardy frontiersmen to be used as scouts against the hostile Indians, to be commanded by yourself, with Lieutenant Beecher, Third Infantry, your subordinate. You can enter into such articles of agreement with these men as will compel obedience.

Forsyth had no problem hiring the frontiersmen at a dollar a day plus 35 cents for use of their horse. The government armed and fed them. 'Our equipment was simple,' he wrote:

> A blanket apiece, saddle and bridle, a lariat and picket-pin, a canteen, a haversack, butcher knife, tin plate and tin cup. A Spencer repeating rifle, a Colt's revolver, army size, and 140 rounds of rifle and 30 rounds of revolver ammunition per man – this carried on the person. In addition, we had a pack-train of four mules carrying camp kettles and picks and shovels, in case it became necessary to dig for water, together with 4,000 extra rounds of ammunition.

At dawn on 17 September 1868, Forsyth's command clashed with hostiles on the Arickaree Fork of the Republican River in Colorado. A combined force of Sioux, Cheyenne and Arapaho attacked the scouts, who hurriedly dug themselves into a shallow defensive position on a small island in the low river. After several unsuccessful advances, the Indians settled to a siege that would last nine days. It was a desperate fight. Chauncey B. Whitney kept a diary during the battle. On the first day, he recorded:

> About 500 attacked us on all sides, with their unearthly yells. The balls flew thick and fast. The colonel was the first man wounded. Lt Beecher was wounded twice, as was the colonel. In a few moments eight or ten were hurt, some fatally. The ground on which our little squad was fighting was sandy . . . With a butcher knife and our hands we soon had a trench which completely covered us from the enemy. Behind the works we fought the red devils all day till dark.

The Indians were well armed with Springfield breech-loaders, Remington rifles, Spencer and Henry repeaters, and plenty of ammunition. When one particular Indian aggravated the injured Forsyth by prancing about, out of range of the Spencers, taunting and insulting the scouts, Forsyth ordered three men, who also had breech-loading Springfields, to sight the rifles at their limit – 1,200yd – and attempt to stop the cavorting warrior. They did.

Frank Harrington had a strange escape from death. He was sent to the north bank of the river to act as sharpshooter with two others. They were all wounded: Harrington by an arrow in the forehead over the left eye. A comrade could not pull it out. But an Indian bullet struck the arrow and knocked it from his head! Harrington recalled the Indian who fired the bullet at him:

> I do not think the Indian saw me until he was almost upon us. He was mounted and coming from the north and he rode almost over me; we both fired at the same time, and we were so near together I am sure I hit him; at the same time the arrow fell to the ground.

There is no doubt that the sustained fire of the Spencers saved the scouts from being overwhelmed. And the death of Roman Nose, war leader of the Cheyenne, took the heart out of the enemy. Forsyth, seriously wounded, recalled the moment in which the chief was killed:

> Riding about five paces in front of the center line and twirling his heavy Springfield rifle . . . Roman Nose recklessly led the charge . . . Sitting upright in my pit as well as I was able, I shouted 'Now! Now!' Instantly the scouts were on their

The fight at Beecher Island, Colorado, in September 1868. Spencer repeating rifles saved Forsyth's scouts from being overrun. (From the painting by Rufus F. Zogbaum, 1901)

knees, with rifles at their shoulders. A quick flash of their eyes along the barrels, and forty good men and true sent their first of seven successive volleys into the ranks of charging warriors.

Forsyth had sent two pairs of scouts for help and they had managed to slip past the Indians. A rescue force appeared on the morning of 25 September. The dead – Lieutenant Beecher, the surgeon and three scouts – were buried on the island, which was named after Beecher. Most of the survivors were wounded. It was difficult to assess Indian casualties as they carried off their dead and wounded.

The Winchester Rifle

The Spencer was also used with devastating effect by Custer's 7th Cavalry against the Indians at the Washita in November 1868. But the Spencer could not compete with its new rival, the seventeen-shot Winchester Model of 1866, and the Spencer Repeating Rifle Company went out of business in 1869.

In 1866, Oliver Winchester reorganised his firearms business, the New Haven Arms Company, as the Winchester Repeating Arms Company and produced a new improved version of the Henry, which had served so well in the Civil War. He called it the Winchester Rifle Model 1866. It had a more convenient and efficient loading system and a less complicated action than the Henry. It had a gleaming brass frame which found favour with Indians and led to the weapon's nickname 'Yellow Boy'. The Model 1866 had a seventeen-cartridge magazine capacity and the carbine thirteen. Failing to obtain military contracts, Winchester promoted his new rifle in the civilian market with considerable success.

The second Winchester, the Model 1873, was basically the same as the earlier model but it was stronger, simpler, and lighter. It had a sliding lid covering the ejection port in the top of the frame to keep dirt and water out of the action. The frame and butt were of forged iron (later of steel) to replace the brass of the Model 1866, and it used a .44–40 centrefire cartridge (.44in or 11.12mm bullet backed by 40 grains of powder), an improved cartridge which gave a substantial increase in range and stopping power over the earlier model's .44in rimfire cartridge of 28 grains.

In the following years the Model 1873 was produced in various barrel lengths and calibres, but the basic shape and mechanism remained unchanged. The quick-firing Winchester carbine, stoutly constructed, easy to operate, was the ideal saddle gun. It was never officially adopted by the US military, the Ordnance Department preferring the single-shot breech-loading Springfield, which served the regular army until 1892, when it was replaced by the Krag-Jorgensen magazine rifle.

The Winchester 1873 enjoyed wide popularity throughout the West, and the world; indeed it was so

The Winchester Model of 1866 had a brass frame that made it attractive to Indians, who often decorated the butt with brass studs, as shown here.

successful that in 1878 the Colt company rechambered a number of its popular .45in (11.43mm) Single Action Army or Peacemaker revolvers to take the same .44–40 cartridge used in the Winchester 1873, so that a man need only carry one type of ammunition for both rifle and revolver. Production of the 1873 continued until 1919, the last one being sold new from the factory in 1924. A total of 720,610 of this model were manufactured. Buffalo Bill Cody was full of praise for the Winchester 1873 and wrote the following testimonial to the company in 1875:

I have been using and have thoroughly tested your latest improved rifle. I pronounce your improved Winchester THE BOSS. Believe me you have the MOST COMPLETE rifle ever made.

Cody was armed with 'the boss' when he fought his celebrated duel with Cheyenne chief Yellow Hand in

Buffalo Bill's duel with Yellow Hand, a Cheyenne chief, in July 1876. Both used Winchesters. Cody killed his man, a deed witnessed by both Indians and soldiers.

Buffalo Bill Cody holding his favourite Winchester Model 1873 rifle.

July 1876 during his service as an army scout. Watched by a column of soldiers, Cody and Yellow Hand, who was armed with a Winchester 1866, rode towards each other and fired at a distance of 30yd apart. Cody killed and scalped the chief, holding the grisly trophy high so that the soldiers could see it. The famed scout shouted 'First scalp for Custer!' – Custer had been killed a few weeks earlier.

The 'Plains' Rifle

A significant weapon of the West was the so-called Plains rifle used by celebrated frontiersmen such as Kit Carson and Jim Bridger and hundreds of lesser known and unsung adventurers of the Great Plains and Rocky Mountains. When the hunters and trappers emerged from the eastern woodlands into the plains and mountains of the trans-Mississippi West they required a shorter, more powerful, firearm than the hunter's traditional 'Kentucky' long rifle. They needed one that was easy to handle on horseback, and with the stopping power to drop the larger game, such as the elk, buffalo and grizzly bear. The Plains rifle fulfilled that requirement.

Evolved largely from the 'Kentucky' rifle and the US Model 1803, the percussion-fired Plains rifle, ranging in calibre from .40–.60in was brought to rugged perfection and fame by the Hawken family of St Louis, Missouri, then a thriving commercial centre known as the 'Gateway to the West', where many expeditions and waggon trains outfitted for the journey across the Great Plains. Jacob Hawken and

Kit Carson's Plains rifle with percussion lock, now in the care of the Colorado Historical Society.

'Kit Carson's Men' carrying plains rifles. (Painting by Charles M. Russell)

his brother Samuel established business in St Louis around 1820 and soon made a reputation as excellent gunmakers: Hawken became synonymous with the finest of Plains rifles.

'KIT' CARSON

Christopher 'Kit' Carson was the Daniel Boone of the Rockies, a trapper, army scout and guide, Indian fighter and soldier. Born in Kentucky in 1809 and raised on the Missouri frontier, Kit gained national renown as chief scout to John C. Fremont, the explorer-soldier dubbed the 'Pathfinder of the West'. John Abbott, a member of Fremont's expedition in 1845, has left us this interesting observation of Kit Carson in camp:

> During this journey I often watched Carson's preparation for the night. A braver man than Kit perhaps never lived . . . but with all this he exercised great caution. While arranging his bed,

his saddle, which he always used as a pillow, was disposed in such a manner as to form a barricade for his head. His pistols, half cocked, were placed above it, and his trusty rifle reposed beneath the blanket by his side, where it was ready for instant use but perfectly protected from the damp. He never exposed himself to the open fire light.

Carson was involved in many Indian fights and suffered several wounds and experienced a number of narrow escapes. At the Green River rendezvous – the trade-meeting of trappers – in 1834 Kit got himself drawn into a gunfight with a huge Frenchman named Shunar, a notorious bully. In this duel on horseback both fired at the same time at close quarters. Shunar's

'The Still Hunt', painted by J. H. Moser in 1888. It was professional white hunters of this type who wiped out the buffalo herds and angered the Indians. They attacked a party of hunters in a post called Adobe Walls in June 1874. (Courtesy of National Park Service, US Department of the Interior)

ball passed through Carson's hair; Kit's slug wounded his opponent's arm. Shunar begged for his life. 'During the remainder of our stay in camp,' Carson said, 'we had no more bother with this French bully.'

THE BUFFALO HUNTERS

The civilisation and religion of the Plains Indians was largely based on the huge, shaggy buffalo which once roamed the Great Plains in millions. For them, hunting was a necessary economic activity. It provided meat, skin for tipis and clothes, and horn and bone for weapons and tools. In the latter half of the nineteenth century, white buffalo hunters began slaughtering the herds for monetary profit. Some

Advertisement for the long-range Sharps buffalo rifle.

'Episode of the Buffalo Gun.' In the fight at Adobe Walls, hunter Billy Dixon, using a powerful Sharps buffalo rifle, knocked an Indian off his horse over a record distance just short of a mile. (From the painting by Frederic Remington)

SHARPS' RIFLES. MODEL 1874.
With Outside Lock and Hammer.

AS OPEN. AS GLOBE.
Beach Combination Sight.
List Price, $2.00.

D

45–100 GRS.
SHARPS CREEDMOOR

On account of the *pressing demands* of Frontiersmen and Buffalo Hunters for **Sharps' Model 1874** Rifles with heavy barrels and double triggers, we were induced to change a *limited number* at considerable expense to conform to their requirements. The barrels are of *best quality* and *workmanship*, and equal to Sharps' high standard of excellence in *every particular*.
These Arms are all being completed, therefore orders varying from the following descriptions cannot be filled.

killed two hundred and fifty a day. By 1870, three million were being slaughtered annually.

The US Military approved. Lt-General Philip Henry Sheridan, Commander of the Military Division of Missouri, was asked if something should be done to stop the mass slaying. He replied: 'Let them kill, skin, and sell until the buffalo is exterminated; it is the only way to bring lasting peace and allow civilisation to advance.' It was a ruthless means of depriving the Indians of their sustenance, making them easier to subdue.

The Sharps rifle proved to be the most efficient death-dealer in the hands of the professional hunters. The classic single-shot buffalo rifle was the .45in calibre model using a 120-grain powder charge and a bullet weighing 550 grains. This load gave the Sharps tremendous stopping power and a supposed range of 1,000yd. Designed for paper or linen cartridges, after the Civil War many early Sharps were converted to fire metallic rimfire and centre-fire cartridges. Buffalo hunters, reliant upon their skill for

'Buffalo Hunt'. Hunters deal with a charging bull using revolvers at close range. (Painting by H. W. Hansen)

a living, and killing so many animals each day, became very proficient, often exceptional marksmen. Some remarkable long-distance shots are recorded with the Sharps – such as Bill Tilghman's which dropped a buffalo at a mile – but the most celebrated long shot of all was made by buffalo hunter Billy Dixon in June 1874, on human prey.

Incensed by the wholesale slaughter of the buffalo, a combined force of Comanche, Cheyenne and Kiowa braves attacked a party of hunters at the Adobe Walls trading post. Marksmanship and the Sharps rifles kept the Indians at bay. On the third day of the siege, Dixon espied a group of Indians far away on a high bluff, seemingly planning another attack. He selected a target, tiny at that range. He sighted his 'Big Fifty' Sharps. He squeezed the trigger. He astonished himself and the other hunters, and definitely the

The Remington rolling-block breech-loader.

Indians. His bullet knocked a brave off his horse. Shortly after the siege was relieved, a US Army surveyor measured the distance from the post to the high bluff – 1,538yd, just 222yd short of the mile.

Another popular buffalo gun and sporting rifle was the Remington rolling-block rifle, a novel type of breech-loader in which the breech-block, when rolled back by the thumb, extracted the spent cartridge case and exposed the chamber. With a fresh cartridge inserted, the shooter rolled the breech-block back into place, ready to fire. George Armstrong Custer was a Remington enthusiast:

> Headquarters Fort Abraham Lincoln, DT
> Messrs Remington & Sons: October 5, 1873
> Dear Sirs,
> Last year I ordered from your firm a Sporting Rifle, caliber .50. I received the rifle a short time prior to the departure of the Yellowstone Expedition [20 June–21 September 1873] . . .
>   The number of animals killed is not so remarkable as the distance at which the shots were executed. The average distance at which the forty-one antelopes were killed was 250 yards by actual measurement. I rarely obtained a shot

at an antelope under 150 yards, while the range extended from that distance up to 630 yards.
>   With the expedition were professional hunters . . . Many of the officers and men also were excellent shots . . . I was the only person who used one of your Rifles . . . I killed far more game than any other single party, professional or amateur, while the shots made with your rifle were at longer range and more difficult shots than were those made by any other rifles in the command . . .

> I am truly yours,
> G. A. Custer,
> Brevet Major-General US Army

By 1883, the rapacious white hunters had brought the buffalo, which had numbered some sixty million in 1800, to the edge of extinction. The species was saved just in time. With the buffalo gone, the Sharps was no longer required. The Sharps Rifle Company never developed a repeating rifle and went out of business in 1881.

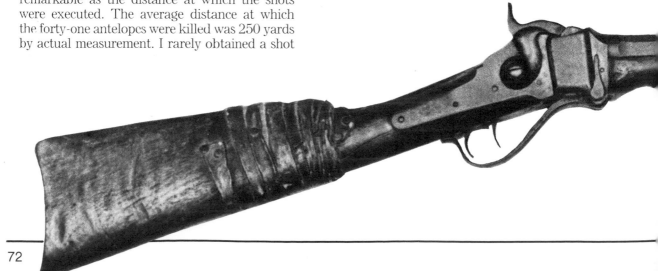

The Sharps rifle used by Bill Tilghman to kill a buffalo at nearly a mile. When the stock of the gun was broken, Bill mended it with a strip of fresh buffalo rawhide which, in drying, made a steel-strong band that remains to this day. Tilghman killed 7,500 buffalo with this gun.

General George A. Custer on campaign with his Indian scouts, who proudly display their Colt 1873 cavalry issue revolvers. Note the Remington rolling-block rifle at Custer's feet.

6
REVOLVERS

In June 1844, about eighty Comanche warriors attacked Captain John Coffee Hays and his fourteen-strong party of Texas Rangers. The Comanches were accustomed to facing single-shot weapons. After the initial burst of gunfire, when the firearms were being reloaded, the Indians would dash in, shooting their arrows. But this time, the braves experienced a deadly shock. Instead of dismounting and taking up a defensive position, Hays led his yelling Rangers in a spirited charge. At close quarters, their new Colt five-shot repeating pistols took a heavy toll.

Stunned by the unexpected firepower, the surviving Comanches fled in terror. More than thirty lay dead. The Rangers suffered several dead and wounded, the latter including Lieutenant Samuel H. Walker.

Colt's revolver saved the Rangers in a number of Indian encounters. Later, when Sam Colt was in financial trouble, the Rangers saved him and his gun: 'Texas has done more for me and my arms,' Colt acknowledged, 'than all the country.'

THE WALKER COLT

Samuel Colt, inventor of the first practical revolving pistol, secured a US Patent on 25 February 1836. It was based on three principles:

Samuel Colt, inventor of the first practical revolving pistol.

1 The cocking of the hammer rotated a multi-chambered breech in a manner which aligned each chamber in succession with a single barrel.
2 The cocking action automatically locked the cylinder in preparation to fire.
3 Each nipple, fitted with a percussion cap, was separated by a partition to ensure the discharge of only that chamber which was in line with the barrel.

Colt set up business at Paterson, New Jersey, where he produced five-shot revolvers, rifles and carbines. His best customer was the Republic of Texas, and he supplied rifles and pistols to the Texas Navy and Army. Nevertheless, the company failed through lack of sales. In 1845, Texas joined the United States, thus sparking off war between the US and Mexico in 1846. Jack Hays became a colonel, and Sam Walker a captain, of the US Regiment of Mounted Riflemen, during the spring and summer of 1846 when the Texas Rangers became part of the US Army. Their bravery and ferocity in battle became legendary; their casual brutality towards anyone Mexican became notorious. An American officer who observed Colonel Hays' Regiment in November 1847 observed: 'Each man carried a rifle, a pair of pistols and one or two of Colt's revolvers . . . A hundred of them could discharge a thousand shots in two minutes.'

A Colt five-shot revolver made at the Paterson plant in New Jersey about 1842, the type used by the Texas Rangers.

Walker wanted an improved Colt revolver for his soldiers. He wrote to Samuel Colt:

The pistols which you made for the Texas Navy have been in use by the Rangers for three years . . . Without your pistols we would not have had the confidence to have undertaken such daring adventures . . . With improvements I think [your pistol] can be rendered the most perfect weapon in the world for light mounted troops.

Captain Walker met with Colt to discuss an order for one thousand revolvers with such alterations and improvements as Walker suggested. Colt was anxious to secure the order, but had no factory of his own, so he arranged with another gunmaker, Eli Whitney Jr, to manufacture the pistols at Whitneyville, Connecticut. The result was the so-called Walker Colt, a .44in (11.22mm) calibre six-shot. Few of these huge 'hand cannons' reached the Rangers in Texas before the fighting with Mexico ended in September 1847, but the new-style sixshooter ensured Sam Colt's fame and fortune. He opened his own factory at Hartford, Connecticut, and produced a successful family of firearms for home and foreign markets. In the American Civil War, the Colt armoury manufactured more than three hundred thousand revolvers and one hundred thousand rifles and muskets.

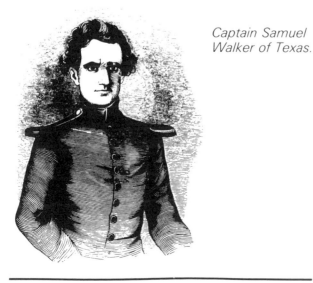

Captain Samuel Walker of Texas.

WILD BILL AND WESTERN GUNFIGHTS

Hollywood has created many myths. One of the most enduring is that of the cowboy gunfight: the ritual quick-draw confrontation, man to man, face to face out in the open, obeying the honourable 'Code of the West'. Only cowards shot a man in the back on the silver screen. In reality, then, there must have been a great deal of cowardice in the old West. Wild Bill Hickok, Jesse James, Pat Garrett and John Wesley Hardin, to name but a few, were all killed by shots in the back.

The movie-makers invented the image of the professional gunfighter wearing a low-slung gun holster, tied to the leg, the supposed 'trade mark' of his calling. In fact, the holster was worn high on the hip. Some real gunmen did not always use holsters and carried their revolvers stuck into a waistbelt, buccaneer fashion. And if they packed a pair of pistols they rarely blazed away with one in each hand in the stereotyped movie manner.

The truth is that a gunman of the old West intent on killing his rival or adversary usually did so covertly: by ambush, trickery or surprise. Shooting a man in the back was far more certain than a risky face-to-face encounter. Pat Garrett gunned down Billy the Kid by surprise in a darkened bedroom. The famed Tom Horn stalked his victims like a hunter, shooting them at long distance.

J. B. Hickok

Not all the legendary gunfighters were craven-hearted. Tricks and treachery apart, the 'shootist' of the old West was usually a man of cool courage, quiet demeanour, and considerable shooting skill. James Butler 'Wild Bill' Hickok is a fine example. Frontiersman, gunfighter and law officer, Hickok's exploits, real and imaginary, have kept writers and movie-makers busy for many years. Some claim that he was probably the greatest of the old time shootists, truly the 'Prince of Pistoleers'.

Hickok himself told Henry M. Stanley, the celebrated journalist-explorer, that he had killed more than a hundred men, but then Hickok was prone to wild exaggeration when the mischievous mood took him. In reality, he killed less than ten. One of his victims was Dave Tutt, whom Wild Bill gunned down in a shoot-out somewhat in the stylised Hollywood manner. It took place on 21 July 1865 in the Market Square of Springfield, Missouri.

The fight started after an argument over a game of poker in which Tutt acquired Hickok's watch, and boasted that he would wear it in the town square as a symbol of his triumph. Wild Bill objected to this strutting and said that he would shoot Tutt if he took such action. But Tutt, himself a good pistol shot, chose to ignore the warning. They confronted each other at a distance of some one hundred paces. Both drew and fired at the same time.

Tutt missed with his shot, then fell dead with a bullet in his heart. An instant later Wild Bill whipped round on Tutt's armed friends and levelled his big Navy Colt at them, saying: 'Aren't you satisfied, gentlemen? Put up your shooting irons, or there'll be more dead men here.' Suitably impressed by Hickok's marksmanship and cool courage, they did not argue the point. Wild Bill stood trial for Tutt's death but was acquitted on his plea of self defence.

Hickok presented a striking figure, being six feet tall with shoulder-length hair in the frontier style. When not in buckskins he dressed in fashionable city clothes. He was quiet and courteous in his manner and speech. According to General George A. Custer, Hickok was not a 'quarrelsome man'. And if we are to believe Hickok himself, he never killed a man except in self defence or in the line of official duty as a lawman. Then why was he dubbed 'Wild Bill'? It has been claimed that he won his famous sobriquet in 1861 by stopping a mob, single-handed, from lynching a man.

Contrary to the Hollywood myth of the flashy quick-draw, lightning speed in drawing a pistol was not the fundamental requisite for survival. Of course, promptness in bringing a gun into action was important, but deliberation (which took a lot of nerve) and accuracy were the prime factors for success in a gunfight. 'Whenever you get into a row be sure and not shoot too quick,' Hickok advocated, 'take time. I've known many a fellow to slip up for shooting in a hurry.' Wyatt Earp, who engaged in several gunfights, also advised that deliberation was the key to survival. The victor in a shootout, he said, would be the one who 'took his time and pulled the trigger once.'

Wild Bill usually wore two revolvers, the Colt Navy Model of 1851, stuck into a belt or silk sash, with the butts forward, which he pulled into action with a peculiar 'twist draw' movement. Being a 'professional' pistoleer Hickok regularly checked the loads of his brace of Navy Colts, cleaning chambers and nipples and inspecting the percussion caps to ensure instant operation. 'When I draw and pull,' he said, 'I must be sure.'

Hickok was undoubtedly a skilled shot. Legend has it that he could cut a chicken's throat with a bullet at thirty paces without breaking its neck, that he could drive the cork into a bottle with a bullet and not break the bottle neck, and that he could hit a dime at fifty paces nine times out of ten. Such tales apart, Hickok knew the gunfighting business and once gave the following advice to a friend:

I hope that you never have to shoot a man, but if you do, shoot him in the guts, near the navel, the broadest target from head to heels. You may not make a fatal shot, but he will get a shock that will paralyse his brain and arm so much that the fight will be over.

Wild Bill Hickok was killed in August 1876 in the town of Deadwood, Dakota Territory, while playing cards. He was shot in the back of the head by the cowardly Jack McCall, who was later hanged for the murder.

The legendary Wild Bill Hickok armed with a brace of Colt Navy Model 1851 percussion revolvers. The knife was probably the photographer's idea to make Bill look more wild. (Courtesy of Kanas State Historical Society)

Colt also produced derringers. This Model No3 was made about 1875.

The Colt Model 1862, a percussion-type six-shot.

The Walker-Colt of 1847, so called because Captain Sam Walker collaborated with Colt in the design. (Photograph courtesy of the J. M. Davis Gun Museum, Claremore, Oklahoma)

The Colt Double Action Model 1878 owned by C. L. 'Gunplay' Maxwell of the Butch Cassidy outlaw gang. (Photograph courtesy of the E. Dixon Larson Collection)

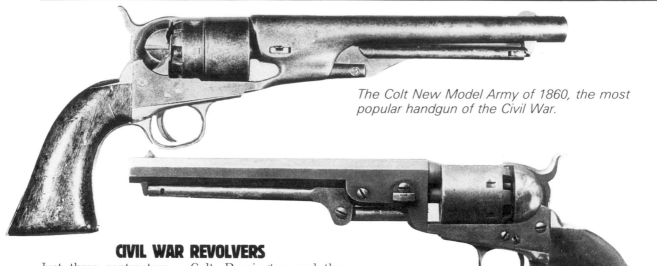

The Colt New Model Army of 1860, the most popular handgun of the Civil War.

The Colt Navy Model 1851 percussion revolver.

CIVIL WAR REVOLVERS

Just three contractors – Colt, Remington and the Starr Arms Company of New York – supplied over 85 per cent of all revolvers ordered by the Federal government during the Civil War. The most popular revolving pistols of the Civil War between the States were those produced by Colt's patent Fire Arms Manufacturing Company of Hartford, Connecticut.

Civil War Colts
Of the various types of Colt revolvers used in the Civil War, the .44in (11.22mm) calibre New Model Army of 1860 was the most successful .and the principal handgun of both Northern and Southern forces. The Federal Ordnance Department purchased 128,697 of the Colt 1860 from 13 April 1861 to 3 April 1866. The Confederates gained their Yankee Colts either by capture or through devious deals. The Colt factory produced 200,000 of this model, including those for civilian sale, from 1860 to 1873. Another notable Civil War Colt was the .36in (9.1mm) calibre Navy Model of 1851. The Federal Ordnance Department bought 11,696 of this model in the period noted above. Colt also produced a five-shot revolving chamber rifle/carbine, but this proved unpopular owing to the unsafe side flash from the chamber and not many were purchased.

Colt's Patent Fire Arms Manufacturing Company at Hartford, Connecticut, as it looked in 1862.

MOSEBY'S RAIDERS

The Colt may have been a Yankee invention, but it was the bold Southern Raiders who demonstrated what could be done with it. Revolvers, especially Colts, were the favoured arms of the mounted Confederate guerrillas. Not for them the traditional edged weapon of cavalry. 'I think I was the first cavalry commander who discarded the sabre as useless . . .' wrote John Singleton Moseby, legendary guerrilla leader. 'My men were as little impressed by a body of cavalry charging with sabres as though they had been armed with cornstalks.' Moseby's Rangers armed themselves with four to six revolvers each. They did not pay for them – they plundered them.

These irregular horsemen – of whom Moseby was the most celebrated and William Clarke Quantrill the most ruthless – were formed to strike at Federal supply and communication lines, thus tying down large numbers of Union troops in guard and escort duties. Moseby's Rangers were exceptional, more like regular cavalry than guerrillas in the traditional manner. Quantrill, on the other hand, was a cruel and brutal killer, his followers including Frank and Jesse James and the Younger brothers. The Federals also carried out guerrilla warfare.

The Colt revolver was ideal for Moseby's style of warfare. Moseby relied upon stealth, surprise and the shock of the mounted charge, with revolvers, against soldiers usually armed with single-shot muzzle-loaders. In April 1863, Moseby and seventy of his men ran into one hundred and fifty Union troopers led by Captain Flint at Miskel's Barn. The Federals fired off their Colts at middle range with little effect, holstered them, and drew sabres for the charge. Moseby's Rangers met them in characteristic style: gripping their reins between their teeth, the Southerners blazed away with a Colt in each hand. They knew that the Colt could be used best at short range, firing by sense of direction in a mêlée. Flint died in total defeat, his command suffering nearly a hundred dead or prisoner, with as many horses and Colt sixshooters falling into enemy hands.

In late 1864, a special campaign was mounted to wipe out Moseby, so great a threat had he become through tying down assets and disruption. Major-General Phil Sheridan sent a crack command of one hundred troopers under 'hardened Indian fighter' Richard Blazer, to seek out and destroy the 'Gray Ghost'. Blazer's men were armed with Spencer repeating rifles. They failed: Moseby's raiders bushwacked the Union troopers and routed them with Colt gunfire.

Confederate irregular cavalry armed with Colt revolvers charging Union infantry.

Colonel John S. Moseby, brilliant Confederate leader of guerrilla horsemen.

The Remington New Model Army of 1863.

The Remington Army Model of 1861. Remington six-shot revolvers rivalled the Colt in popularity.

The original deringer made by Henry Deringer of Philadelphia. When other gunmakers began to produce similar models, all pocket pistols came to be known as 'derringers', spelt with a double 'r'.

A Remington double-barrelled derringer, a popular pocket pistol.

Samuel Colt, born in 1814, died in January 1862, but lived long enough to enjoy the explosion of business generated by the American Civil War, as the following contracts addressed to him at Hartford, Connecticut, attest:

Ordnance Officer, Washington,
June 12, 1861

Sir,

Please furnish this department, as soon as possible, with five thousand Colt's revolver pistols, of the latest pattern. The pistols are to undergo inspection, and the price [$25 each] will be the same as allowed for the same kind of pistols recently furnished by you.

James W. Ripley,
Lieutenant-Colonel of Ordnance

Ordnance Officer, Washington,
September 17, 1861

Sir,

Deliver weekly, until further orders, as many of your pistols, holsters, new pattern, as you can make.

James W. Ripley
Brigadier-General

A Remington New Model Army of 1863, to which a trigger different from that of the factory-made model has been fitted. An unusual conversion.

Remington

E. Remington and Sons were highly regarded in the Wild West as manufacturers of revolvers and rifles, and as Colt's main competitor. The company also produced a successful range of derringer pocket pistols. Founded by gunsmith Eliphalet Remington in 1816, the company produced its first revolver in 1857, a model designed by Fordyce Beals, a pocket pistol for civilian use.

Beals then designed a larger revolver with a new type of loading lever and cylinder pin and this developed into the Remington Model 1861, made in .44in (11.22mm) calibre for the Army and .36in (9.1mm) calibre for the Navy. Further improvements resulted in the New Model Army of 1863, so successful that it was second only to the Colt Model 1860 in popularity during the Civil War. More than one hundred and twenty-nine thousand Remingtons were purchased by the Ordnance Department between 13 April 1861 and 3 April 1866.

AMERICAN REVOLVERS OF THE 1870s

The Peacemaker

The most celebrated of all Colts is without doubt the Single Action Army Revolver, Model 1873, in .45in (11.43mm) calibre – the Peacemaker model. All Colt revolvers before this model wcrc percussion type: loaded with separate lead balls and powder and fired by percussion cap. With the perfection of the metal cartridge, in which cap, powder and ball were enclosed in a single metal case, firearm manufacture was revolutionised and a whole new line of Colt and other revolvers was produced, of which the Peacemaker became the most famous and enduring. It is still manufactured today.

The Colt Model of 1873 was adopted by the US Army and also sold widely in the open market, manufactured in various barrel lengths and calibres. It is the type mostly seen in Western movies.

A cowboy using a Single Action Colt Peacemaker.
(From the painting *'Hard Pushed'* by Charles Schreyvogel)

The Remington New Model Army of 1875 and gunbelt used by Frank James (brother of Jesse), who wrote and signed the attestation displayed with the gun. (Photograph courtesy of the Frontier Museum Historical Center, Temecula, California)

Bartholomew 'Bat' Masterson, noted law officer, gambler and gunfighter, purchased eight .45in Peacemakers directly from the Colt company during the period 1879–85. He knew exactly what he required in a handgun, as detailed in the following letter written to the Colt company on 24 July 1885, while he was staying in Dodge City, Kansas:

> Gents,
> Please send me one of your nickle plated short .45 caliber revolvers. It is for my own use and for that reason I would like to have a little extra paines taken with it. I am willing to pay extra for extra work. Make it very easy on [the] trigger and have the front sight a little higher and thicker than the ordinary pistol of this kind. Put on a gutta percha [hard rubber] handle and send it as soon as possible. Have the barrel about the same length that the ejecting rod is [4¾in].
> Truly yours
> W. B. Masterson

It is noteworthy that he should be so interested in a sight on a revolver, and in ensuring a good gripping surface for the butt to allow steady aim. Masterson clearly believed in 'taking time'.

Two years later, Remington produced their cartridge model of 1875. It too had its aficionado. Frank James, brother of Jesse, preferred a Remington and extolled the weapon as 'the hardest and surest shooting pistol made.'

Smith & Wesson

The Smith & Wesson company also produced six-shooters popular in frontier times. These revolvers of the 1870s differed mainly from those of Colt and Remington in that they had a break-open, tip-up action that ejected all the spent cartridges simultaneously as the cylinder and barrel cleared the frame. In contemporary Colts and Remingtons, the empty cases had to be pushed out one by one with the ejector rod attached to the barrel. Horace Smith and Daniel Wesson produced their first revolver in 1857, a small .22in (5.58mm) calibre seven-shot. When Samuel L. Clemens, alias Mark Twain, journeyed to the Far West as a young man in 1861, he armed himself with a Smith & Wesson. In his account of his Western travels, *Roughing It*, published in 1872, he wrote:

> I was armed to the teeth with a pitiful little Smith & Wesson's seven-shooter, which carried a ball like a homeopathic pill, and it took the whole seven to make a dose for an adult. But I thought it was grand. It appeared to me to be a dangerous

SCIENTIFIC AMERICAN

A WEEKLY JOURNAL OF PRACTICAL INFORMATION, ART, SCIENCE, MECHANICS, CHEMISTRY AND MANUFACTURES

NEW YORK, JANUARY 24, 1880.

Front page of the Scientific American *of 24 January 1880, showing scenes in the Smith & Wesson revolver factory.*

The Schofield Smith & Wesson used by Jesse James.

weapon. It only had one fault – you could not hit anything with it.

In 1870, Smith & Wesson introduced their Model No3, also known as the American Model, a .44in (11.22mm) calibre centrefire six-shot. The army tested it, liked it and ordered a thousand. This revolver also impressed the Russian government which, with slight alterations for military use, ordered twenty thousand for army service. When George Schofield of the Tenth Cavalry contributed certain modifications to No3, the Schofield Smith & Wesson was born. The US Army purchased 8,285 of the modified model and several security express companies armed their guards and agents with them.

In 1890, the Director of the US Census stated in his report that 'there can hardly be said to be a frontier line.' The Wild West days were virtually over. The Dalton brothers were among the last of the old-style horse-riding outlaws. Born in Missouri, Robert, Grattan and Emmett Dalton were kin to the Younger brothers who rode with Jesse James. In October 1892, the Daltons and two others rode into Coffeyville, Kansas, to rob the bank. As the gang attempted to escape from the bank, a fierce shoot-out ensued with the angry citizens. When the gunsmoke cleared, four robbers lay dead. A fifth, Emmett Dalton, was badly wounded. Four citizens had been killed and three wounded. Emmett Dalton recovered and was sentenced to life imprisonment for murder. Released after fourteen years, he emerged into the twentieth century, a reformed man. He became a respectable businessman and died in 1937.

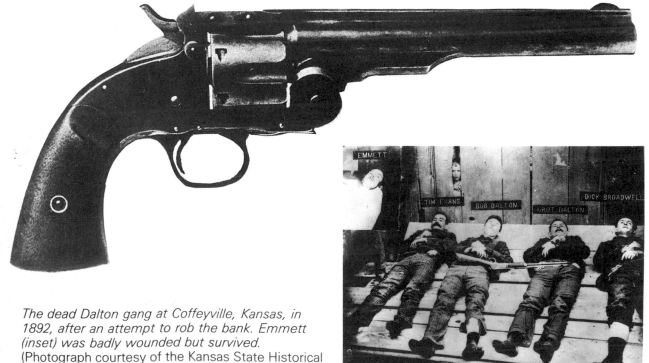

The dead Dalton gang at Coffeyville, Kansas, in 1892, after an attempt to rob the bank. Emmett (inset) was badly wounded but survived.
(Photograph courtesy of the Kansas State Historical Society)

A British sapper, during the Indian Mutiny of 1857, waiting in a mine for an enemy counter-sapper to break through. He holds a Colt revolver cocked for action.

BRITISH REVOLVERS

When Sam Colt's revolvers were displayed at the Great Exhibition at Crystal Palace in 1851, they created a great deal of interest. Sam Colt, visiting London to attend the exhibition, capitalised on the interest by opening a London factory in 1853. Colt revolvers became popular with British officers, who used them in the Crimean War of 1854–6, the Indian Mutiny of 1857–8, and various colonial campaigns. The War Office purchased a large number of Colts for the Army and Royal Navy.

Colt, however, had a London rival in Robert Adams who had patented a double-action revolver in February 1851, a weapon as good as, if not superior to, the Colt. Adams claimed that his solid-framed revolver was stronger than the Colt, that its bigger bore of .50in (12.7mm) delivered greater stopping power than the popular .36in (9.1mm) Colt Navy Model of 1851, and that the Adams double-action made it a faster-firing weapon in close combat. The Colt was single-action, that is, the hammer had to be thumb cocked for each shot, whereas a single pull on the Adams trigger cocked the hammer, rotated the cylinder, and released the hammer to fire the shot. The battle benefit of the double-action or self-cocking system was stressed in a letter to Robert Adams from J. G. Crosse of the 88th Regiment in the Crimea:

> I had one of your largest-sized Revolver Pistols at the bloody battle of Inkermann, and by some

Robert Adams, the English gun designer, loading the Adams percussion revolver.

An engraved Adams revolver complete with accessories.

chance got surrounded by Russians. I then found the advantages of your pistol over that of Colonel Colt's, for had I to cock before each shot I should have lost my life. I should not have had time to cock, as they were too close to me . . . so close that I was bayonetted through the thigh immediately after shooting the fourth man.

In 1855, Robert Adams improved his gun by incorporating the mechanism invented by Lieutenant Beaumont, Royal Engineers, which allowed for either single or double-action. The Beaumont-Adams pistol was adopted by Her Majesty's Government for official service use.

William Tranter, another British gunsmith, patented his revolver in 1853. The Tranter featured two triggers: one to cock the hammer, the other to fire it. Tranter later produced an improved model with single trigger and double-action. The Tranter proved to be an excellent weapon and in 1858 was taken up by the government. In 1863, Tranter was the first British gunmaker to patent a breech-loading rimfire revolver, using a cartridge with the detonating mixture in the rim, or flange, at the base.

The Webley

The most celebrated of British military revolvers is the Webley, the British Army's handgun for more than seventy years. The Birmingham company of Philip Webley & Son produced a revolver in 1882

that featured a break-open frame for simultaneous self-ejection of used cartridges, similar to that of the American Smith & Wesson action. It was officially described as 'six chambered, top opening with automatic extraction.' It was this .455m calibre weapon, with its substantial improvements, that secured the initial army order for ten thousand revolvers in 1887. The revolver entered service in November 1897. It is interesting to note that their actual calibre is .441in. (11.20mm).

Ten years and four models later, Webley merged with W. & C. Scott and Son to become the Webley & Scott Revolver Arms Co Ltd in 1897, shortened in 1906 to Webley & Scott Ltd. The Webley Mark 4 was standard issue for British troops in the Boer War, and, together with the Mark 5 and 6, served throughout World War One. Some three hundred thousand Mark 6s were delivered. Webley & Scott also produced a semi-automatic pistol for war service. The Webley is among the most accurate and strongest handguns ever made, which, together with the quality of the materials used and the standard of workmanship has ensured that many are still in service.

In 1881, the Royal Small Arms Factory (RSA) at Enfield Lock had produced a service revolver that proved unsatisfactory; a Webley design replaced it. In the 1920s, the RSA tried again and eventually produced the Revolver No2 Mark I in .38in (9.65mm) calibre, of which the army purchased large numbers

WEBLEY REVOLVERS AND PISTOLS.

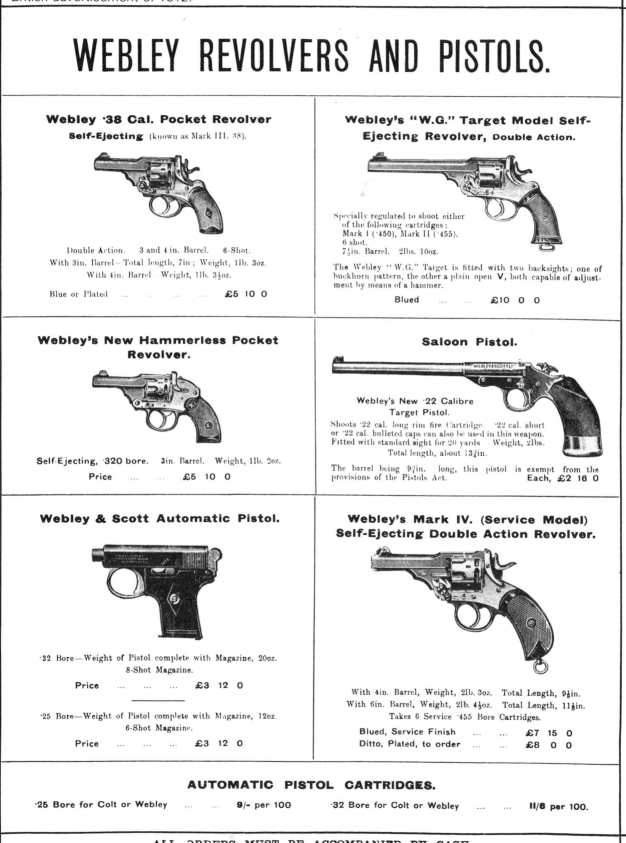

Webley ·38 Cal. Pocket Revolver

Self-Ejecting (known as Mark III. 38).

Double Action.   3 and 4 in. Barrel.   6-Shot.
With 3in. Barrel – Total length, 7in ; Weight, 1lb. 3oz.
With 4in. Barrel – Weight, 1lb. 3½oz.

Blue or Plated **£5 10 0**

Webley's "W.G." Target Model Self-Ejecting Revolver, **Double Action.**

Specially regulated to shoot either
of the following cartridges :
Mark I (·450), Mark II (·455).
6 shot.
7½in. Barrel.   2lbs. 10oz.

The Webley "W.G." Target is fitted with two backsights; one of buckhorn pattern, the other a plain open **V**, both capable of adjustment by means of a hammer.

Blued **£10 0 0**

Webley's New Hammerless Pocket Revolver.

Self-Ejecting, ·320 bore.   3in. Barrel.   Weight, 1lb. 2oz.
Price **£5 10 0**

Saloon Pistol.

Webley's New ·22 Calibre Target Pistol.

Shoots ·22 cal. long rim fire Cartridge.   ·22 cal. short or ·22 cal. bulleted caps can also be used in this weapon.
Fitted with standard sight for 20 yards   Weight, 2lbs.
Total length, about 13¾in.

The barrel being 9¾in. long, this pistol is exempt from the provisions of the Pistols Act.   **Each, £2 16 0**

Webley & Scott Automatic Pistol.

·32 Bore—Weight of Pistol complete with Magazine, 20oz.
8-Shot Magazine.

Price **£3 12 0**

·25 Bore—Weight of Pistol complete with Magazine, 12oz.
6-Shot Magazine.

Price **£3 12 0**

Webley's Mark IV. (Service Model) Self-Ejecting Double Action Revolver.

With 4in. Barrel, Weight, 2lb. 3oz.   Total Length, 9½in.
With 6in. Barrel, Weight, 2lb. 4½oz.   Total Length, 11⅜in.
Takes 6 Service ·455 Bore Cartridges.

Blued, Service Finish **£7 15 0**
Ditto, Plated, to order **£8 0 0**

AUTOMATIC PISTOL CARTRIDGES.

·25 Bore for Colt or Webley   ...   ...   **9/- per 100**   ·32 Bore for Colt or Webley   ...   ...   **11/6 per 100.**

ALL ORDERS MUST BE ACCOMPANIED BY CASH.

during World War Two. It was actually based upon a Webley design.

The requirement for the new gun was based upon interpreting experience gained by the British Army during World War One. It had been found that the .455in bullet required a weapon which was too heavy for convenience and agility, and which demanded too much skill in firing for the average soldier, especially a wartime-trained man. The army cast around for replacements. In 1923, Webley & Scott designed a .38in (9.65mm) calibre revolver which they tested as a potential police weapon. The 200-grain (12.7gm) bullet which it used, gave the killing power required of a combat weapon, but the pistol was easily enough handled for 'hostilities-only' recruits to be sufficiently accurate. The RSA took over the pistol's development in 1926–7. A number of changes were made in the lockwork and trigger mechanism and the pistol was therefore designated as an Enfield weapon: the Pistol, Revolver, Enfield, Number 2. This explains the apparent paradox of two similar revolvers known by different names, the .45 Webley and the .38 Enfield.

The .38 Enfield could be operated as a single- or double-action weapon: it had a hammer mechanism with a comb to allow the thumb to cock it. The Mark I was introduced to service in June 1932. In June 1938, the Mark I* was introduced. Simultaneously, all Mark Is were withdrawn and converted to Mark I*. The Mark I* differed from the Mark I principally in having the hammer-comb and bent removed to allow double-action firing only: this was done because it had been found that the hammer-comb fouled internal fittings in tanks. The trigger pull was also reduced by lightening the mainspring. The Mark I* was favoured by special forces, rangers and commandos as a 'quick draw and fire' weapon. The wartime Mark I** was introduced in July 1942. It had the hammer safety stop removed, plus some minor adjustments. This was an unpopular modification, as the pistols were somewhat unsafe if dropped. They were withdrawn after the war, and hammer safety stops fitted.

Webley & Scott also produced a model of their own 1923 .38in police design, differing in detail externally and in having a Webley not Enfield lock mechanism. It was designated Pistol, Revolver, Webley 0.38in Mark 4, and was in service from 1942. Revolvers remained in army service until replaced by the Browning semi-automatic pistol in the 1950s.

FIGHTING WITH A PISTOL

Although the occasions in war combat when a pistol would be likely to be used are rare, the object must be quick and accurate shooting. Success in pistol fighting demands constant and realistic practice in accuracy and speed of firing the pistol, and exercises to strengthen the gripping muscles of both hands to ensure rapid draw and steady aim. Effective shooting

is always based on the characteristics of the weapon being used. The British Army's pistol's short barrel necessitates normally firing at close range – 15yd or under – although fire effect may be obtained up to 50yd if cover is used. When fighting in enclosed country (eg villages, woods, trench systems, etc) surprise targets can be very quickly engaged with a pistol. At close range men shoot instantly by sense of direction. Under such conditions the firer is aided by a pistol's high rate of fire, because the speed with which one or more effective shots can be fired then becomes more important than the close grouping of the shots.

To fight with the pistol, men must be trained to think quickly and to act with determination and initiative in order to outwit an enemy. They must be taught and must practise the use of either hand, including using trench systems or buildings for handling the pistol in cramped localities. The ability to fire equally effectively with either hand is a great advantage, because when working round cover, the pistol may be carried in the outside hand so that an opponent can be killed without exposing more than the firer's hand and head. A change of direction will necessitate cleanly and quickly changing hands.

There are three common faults in firing: anticipat-

Webley revolvers served British soldiers throughout World War One. In November 1914 Captain Butler led a party of native troops against German-commanded black soldiers in the German West African colony, the Cameroons. Using his Webley with great effect, Butler defeated the enemy and captured a machine gun.

ing the shock of discharge which causes low scattered shooting; loosening the grip, causing scattered shooting; and failing to release the trigger completely after each shot, which will prevent the mechanism from functioning correctly.

To adopt the 'ready' position, the official British army teaching was

Draw the pistol from the case and bring it in front of the body, muzzle pointing to the front, forefinger on the trigger. Advance either foot slightly. The knees should be slightly bent, with the weight of the body forward. The body must be square to the target, and the hand and pistol be held in the centre of the body. The position of the feet is immaterial. The butt of the pistol must be gripped as firmly as possible and so held that when the pistol is raised it is in alignment with the target for direction . . . The position must be one of aggression and determination. To 'rest', straighten the knees and relax the body, holding the pistol with the muzzle pointing to the front and not to the ground.

When firing from the 'ready' position, concentrate on the centre of the target. Grip the pistol butt as firmly as possible. Raise it quickly in front of the centre of the body, keeping the arm slightly bent. The height to which it is raised depends on the range. At point blank range (under 10yd), it need not be raised above the waist; beyond that, it needs to be raised higher. Fire two shots in quick succession, then return to the ready position. When working round cover, hold the pistol in the outside hand to ensure the minimum of exposure.

On most occasions, the necessity for speed will mean that the pistol will be fired by sense of direction. Shooting by sense of direction requires the attention of the firer to be concentrated on his target the whole time. The firer must face his opponent squarely, determined to kill him. To make certain of killing, two shots must always be fired in quick succession – more if necessary to ensure death.

Golden rules of combat are that the firer should count each round as he fires it to ensure that he will know when to reload; that one should reload a pistol whenever opportunity arises; and never resume an advance with less than two or three live rounds in the cylinder. It was a simple matter to load the .38 or .45 service revolver. Keeping the barrel pointing downwards and to the front, the pistol was opened. Holding the cylinder with the left hand to prevent it rotating, one round was placed in the 10 o'clock chamber, then the other chambers were filled anti-clockwise. The pistol was closed by bringing the butt gently up to the barrel.

Under some circumstances, such as when it is possible to use both hands when firing from cover, it may be desirable to aim the pistol. The principles of using cover are the same as with the rifle. The firing hand or wrist should be gripped with the other hand, and the elbows rested if possible. The rules of aiming a pistol are similar to those for the rifle. Most have an upright foresight and a 'U' backsight. Close the left eye; bring the sights up onto the centre of the target with the backsight upright; and position the top of the foresight in the middle of the 'U' in line with the shoulders of the backsight. When the target is moving across the front, aim at its front edge.

An FBI agent in the prone position at the 60yd firing line of the practical pistol course on the FBI range at Quantico, Virginia.

Chicago policeman Arthur Olson in action during a shoot-out with bank robbers in February 1947. Wounded in the jaw by flying glass, Olson continued firing his Colt revolver until the gunfight ended with two bandits dead and three under arrest.

7
ROOSEVELT
AND THE
ROUGH RIDERS

Theodore Roosevelt was a most remarkable US President. A cultured man of letters, he was also a man of vigorous activity with a wide experience of firearms as rancher, soldier and big-game hunter. His life (1858–1919) spanned a significant period of small-arms history. 'Teddy' was a hunting, shooting enthusiast all his colourful days. He owned more than fifty guns and he triggered virtually every kind of sporting firearm available in his time.

Born of a wealthy family in New York City, Roosevelt was a sickly child, but learned to ride, shoot, swim and box and became an ardent advocate of the strenuous life. After graduating from Harvard in 1880, he entered politics. In September 1883, he made his first visit to the Dakota Badlands to hunt buffalo and other big game, and while there he purchased a ranch.

His trip out West was a resounding success and he became enamoured of the wilderness and the self-reliant Westerners. Returning to New York, he was

Theodore Roosevelt in 1885 holding his favourite Winchester Model 1876 with half-magazine, and gold oval insert in the butt engraved with a bear.

elected to the State Assembly in November 1883. He soon went West again and by August 1885, he had 1,600 head of cattle. He experienced the dangers of Western life. He rode through a stormy night to break up a stampede. He flattened with his fists a drunken and armed desperado who threatened him in a saloon. He trailed and arrested, at gunpoint, a band of robbers. He witnessed gunfights. In *Ranch Life and the Hunting Trail*, 1888, he describes one:

I was once staying in a town where a desperately plucky fight took place. A noted desperado, an Arkansas man, had become involved in a quarrel with two others of the same ilk, both Irishmen and partners. For several days all three lurked about the saloon-infested streets . . . each trying to 'get the drop' – that is, the first shot – the other inhabitants looking forward to the fight with pleased curiosity, no one dreaming of interfering. At last one of the partners got a chance at his opponent as the latter was walking into a gambling hell, and broke his back [with a shot] near the hips; yet the crippled, mortally wounded man twisted around as he fell and shot his slayer dead. Then, knowing that he had but a few moments to live, and expecting that his other foe would run up on hearing the shooting, he dragged himself by his arms out into the street; immediately afterwards, as he anticipated, the second partner appeared, and was killed on the spot. The victor did not live twenty minutes. As in most of these encounters, all of the men who were killed deserved their fate.

Roosevelt and companion arrest some robbers out West. (Illustration by Frederic Remington for Roosevelt's *Ranch Life and the Hunting Trail,* published in 1888)

Roosevelt in his cowboy days wearing a Colt Single Action Frontier model with ivory grips.

In his ranching years Roosevelt witnessed a
number of desperate gunfights such as this one.
(Painting by Charles M. Russell)

'Stalking Goats.' Roosevelt (on left) hunting the
white mountain goat with his favourite Winchester.
(Illustration by Frederic Remington for *Ranch Life
and the Hunting Trail*)

The disastrous winter of 1886–7 wiped out Roosevelt's cattle. He suffered great financial loss. He returned to New York to concentrate on politics. From 1897 to 1898 he held the post of Assistant Secretary of the Navy. When trouble brewed between the US and Spain over the insurrection in Cuba, then a Spanish possession, the battleship USS *Maine* was sent to the island to protect American lives and interests. On 15 February 1898, an underwater explosion sank her off Havana, with the loss of 253 men.

It may have been the hostile Spaniards; it may have been intriguing Cuban rebels who wished to embroil the US in war with Spain who sank the *Maine*; but a US Naval court of enquiry was unable to obtain evidence fixing the sinking on any person or persons. Nevertheless, war fever gripped the American public. After fruitless diplomatic exchanges, Spain and the US declared war in April 1898. Roosevelt was a keen advocate of this war. Ambitious, physically brave and full of energy, he saw a splendid opportunity (probably his last chance) to win personal military glory in combat.

The US Army was unprepared for the Spanish-American War being short of trained men, equipment and supplies and with armouries full of obsolete weapons and ammunition. The regular army was issued with the newly adopted .30in (7.62mm) calibre Krag-Jorgensen bolt-action magazine rifle, developed by Colonel Krag, director of the Kongsberg Arsenal, Norway, and Eric Jorgensen, the plant superintendent. But the militia and volunteer units carried the single-shot .45in (11.43mm) Springfield Model 1873. Regulations allowed a certain latitude in the choice of personal pistols, a popular type in the Spanish-American conflict being the double-action .38in (9.65mm) calibre Colt Model 1892 six-shot revolver.

THE ROUGH RIDERS

When Congress authorised the recruitment of three volunteer cavalry regiments in the West and South West, Roosevelt resigned his navy post and immediately offered to raise one. As previously mentioned, Teddy much admired the cowboy type: 'In all the world,' he wrote, 'there could not be better material for soldiers than that offered by these grim hunters of the mountains, these wild rough riders of the plains.' Roosevelt's regiment of cowboy cavalry was recruited principally from Arizona, New Mexico, Texas, and the Indian Territory (Oklahoma). Officially designated the First US Volunteer Cavalry, newspapers dubbed the outfit the 'Rough Riders' and the term came into official use.

Roosevelt often shot the fleet-footed pronghorn antelope for meat in the pot.

(above) *US regular troops armed with the Krag rifle engage Spanish soldiers in Cuba.* (Illustration by Rufus F. Zogbaum)

(below) *Roosevelt, in the centre, pictured with his Rough Riders in the United States.*

Roosevelt was offered the colonelcy of the regiment but had the good sense, owing to his lack of military experience, to refuse. He proposed that his friend Leonard Wood, a veteran soldier and holder of the Medal of Honor, be made colonel while he, Roosevelt, served as second-in-command. Later during the Cuban campaign Wood took charge of a brigade and Teddy was left in full command of the Rough Riders. Using his considerable influence Roosevelt managed to get his men issued with the Krag-Jorgensen. In *The Rough Riders*, 1899, he wrote:

> Our arms were the regular cavalry carbine, the 'Krag,' a splendid weapon, and the revolver. A few carried their favourite Winchesters, using, of course, the new model which took the government cartridge. We felt very strongly that it would be worse than a waste of time to try to train our men to use the saber – a weapon utterly alien to them; but with the rifle and revolver they were already thoroughly familiar.

The new model Winchester referred to was that of 1895, which differed radically from all preceding Winchesters in that the cartridges were contained in a single column box magazine of military type, instead of the traditional tubular magazine under the barrel. The first Model 95s were chambered for the US Army (.30–40 Krag) cartridge, essentially a smokeless cartridge. Later issues were chambered for a variety of cartridges and offered in carbine and rifle versions. A total of 425,881 Winchester 1895s were manufactured before the model was discontinued in 1931.

Westerners of all types flocked to join the Rough Riders: cowboys, hunters, bronco-busters, Indians, and peace officers. William Owen 'Bucky' O'Neill, a former sheriff of renown, had resigned as Mayor of Prescott, Arizona, to become captain of 'A' Troop. When O'Neill left to join the Rough Riders the entire populace turned out to wish him well and the new mayor made a speech, which, awful though it is to modern understanding, reflected the bellicose spirit of the times:

> As you are going into the cavalry branch of the service, captain, the city is desirous of seeing you properly mounted and they wish to present you with another mount. It is not yet fully grown, being only a *Colt*, but we know that in your hands it will become a warhorse of renown. All you need do is to take the bridle off every time it bucks and head it toward a Spaniard and you can be sure that one more of the enemy will say 'good morning' to his godfather, the Devil.

Thereupon the mayor handed O'Neill a gleaming new Colt revolver.

The USS Maine *blows up in Havana harbour, Cuba, in April 1898, and prompts the United States to declare war on Spain.*

Roosevelt, second from right in dark shirt, in war conference with other officers in Cuba. He wears a flap holster containing the Colt revolver recovered from the sunken Maine. *(Photograph courtesy of The Theodore Roosevelt Collection, Harvard College Library)*

RECOVERING THE DEAD BODIES.

The regiment assembled at San Antonio, Texas, prior to leaving for embarkation at Tampa, Florida, on 30 May 1898. The *San Antonio Express* reported that

> The Rough Riders presented a very warlike appearance as they strolled about the depot before leaving. Their belts were loaded with ammunition, and their carbines and six-shooters were slung in their belts, ready for action.

The regiment collected another nickname, 'Teddy's Terrors'. When the Rough Riders landed in Cuba they fought dismounted, having left their horses behind because of a shortage of transport ships. Only the officers' mounts were taken to Cuba. The regiment first saw action at Las Guasimas, on the road to Santiago, and suffered eight killed and thirty-one wounded. Tom Isbell, a half-breed Cherokee, was probably the first Rough Rider to fire a shot in combat; two minutes later he received the first of seven wounds in the space of thirty minutes. Up to receiving the last wound, Isbell refused to leave the firing line, then loss of blood forced the brave Indian to the rear. Roosevelt recorded that:

> The denseness of the jungle and the fact that [the enemy] used absolutely smokeless powder made it exceedingly difficult to place exactly where they were . . . The effect of the smokeless powder was remarkable. The air seemed full of the rustling sound of the Mauser bullets . . . At every halt we took advantage of the cover, sinking down behind any mound, bush, or tree trunk in the neighborhood. The trees, of course, furnished no protection from the Mauser bullets. Once I was standing behind a large palm with my head out to one side, very fortunately; for a bullet passed through the palm, filling my left eye and ear with the dust and splinters.

On 1 July 1898 Roosevelt's regiment took part in the celebrated action to take the San Juan heights, a fortified ridge in front of Santiago. This was Teddy's 'crowded hour,' as he called it. On horseback, fully exposed to heavy fire, with his Colt Model 1892 six-shooter in hand, he led his pedestrian Rough Riders, and various units of other regiments, up Kettle Hill, a height separate from the main ridge. He described the fight in *The Rough Riders*:

> Lieutenant Davis's first sergeant, Clarence Gould, killed a Spanish soldier with his revolver, just as this Spaniard was aiming at one of my Rough Riders. At about the same time I also shot one. I was with Henry Bardshar [his orderly] running up at the double, and two Spaniards leaped from the trenches and fired at us, not ten yards away. As they turned to run I closed in and fired twice, missing the first and killing the second. My revolver was from the sunken battle-

ship *Maine*, and had been given me by my brother-in-law, Captain W. S. Cowles, of the Navy.

The troopers stormed the hill and captured it. Roosevelt had won the military glory he desired. The Rough Riders suffered heavy casualties. At San Juan Hill some eight thousand five hundred US soldiers attacked frontally an entrenched enemy five hundred strong. The Spaniards were armed with the excellent German Mauser Model 1893 bolt-action rifle in 7mm (.276in) calibre, firing a smokeless cartridge contained in a five-shot magazine. The Mauser proved far superior to the US Krag rifle and ended the latter's service with the US military. The resulting new Springfield Model 1903 was largely inspired by the German rifle. A Mauser messenger of death took the

life of Bucky O'Neill, as Roosevelt relates:

The most serious loss that I and the regiment could have suffered befell just before we charged. Bucky O'Neill was strolling up and down in front of his men, smoking a cigarette . . . He had a theory that an officer ought never to take cover [in front of his men] . . . As O'Neill moved to and fro, his men begged him to lie down, and one of the sergeants said, 'Captain, a bullet is sure to hit you.' O'Neill took his cigarette out of his mouth, and blowing out a cloud of smoke laughed and said, 'Sergeant, the Spanish bullet isn't made that will kill me.' A little later . . . As he turned on his heel a bullet struck him in the mouth and came out at the back of his head.

Bucky O'Neill was buried at Arlington National Cemetery on 1 May 1899. Eight years later a splendid equestrian statue of O'Neill in Rough Rider uniform, by Solon Borglum, was dedicated to his memory in the Plaza at Prescott. Teddy Roosevelt returned home a national hero and went on to become Governor of New York. He was elected US Vice-President in 1900. He succeeded the assassinated President McKinley the following year and remained in office till 1909. He died in 1919.

The victorious Rough Riders stand with their colonel on San Juan Hill, having taken the fortified height from the Spanish.

Lieutenant-Colonel Theodore Roosevelt of the 1st US Volunteer Cavalry, known as the Rough Riders.

Infantry soldier armed with US magazine bolt-action rifle Model 1896, the 'Krag'. (Illustration by Frederic Remington)

The bronze statue by Solon Borglum that stands at Prescott, Arizona, commemorating Captain William 'Bucky' O'Neill of Roosevelt's Rough Riders, killed in Cuba. (Photograph courtesy of Jane Carter's Camera Center, Prescott, Arizona)

Song sheet of 1898 reflecting Roosevelt's popularity as a war hero.

PART THREE
MODERN
GUNS

8
MAXIMS AND MODERN WARFARE

Hiram Maxim's favourite demonstration of his gun's destructive firepower was to cut down a tree with a stream of bullets. Maxim, extreme right, in company with a Chinese envoy.

One day in the late 1880s Hiram Maxim sat behind his revolutionary machine gun that could fire more than 600 rounds a minute. The King of Denmark and officers of his General Staff looked on. Maxim was about to demonstrate the destructive power of his automatic gun. The inventor fired at a stalwart tree and cut it down in a cloud of splinters with a roaring, traversing stream of bullets. It was Maxim's favourite sales promotion stunt. 'To see the bullets making a clean cut across the trunk and to soon witness the fall of the tree,' Maxim wrote, 'was a spectacle that invariably seemed to fully drive home a sense of my gun's ability.'

The Danish monarch was indeed impressed by the performance, but on learning that the weapon ate up cartridges at the rapid rate of £5 a minute (equivalent then to about $25) he commented: 'A most excellent gun, Mr Maxim, but its costly appetite would bankrupt my little kingdom in a few hours.' And when the Maxim was demonstrated to the Chinese envoy, Li Hung Chang, his reaction was similar: 'That won't do for China, it's much too expensive in ammunition.'

But the major European powers, not short of money, or enemies, purchased Maxim's deadly gun and later manufactured it under licence. The Maxim gun was a truly epoch-making weapon, the precursor of a new breed of heavy machine guns which, secure in prepared positions, proved virtually impregnable against traditional infantry attacks unless their sandbagged emplacements or concrete strongpoints were first reduced by accurate and prolonged artillery bombardment.

The Maxim gun, and its variants, changed the face of war. It influenced infantry tactics, instigated the adoption of barbed wire and trench warfare, gave impetus to the design and improvement of artillery and small arms, and, it can be said, inspired the development of the battle tank. The history-making gunfire of Maxim-type guns has echoed round the world for more than a century.

EARLY MACHINE GUNS

Until the advent of the Maxim in 1883, all machine guns were non-automatic, as explained in an article published in the 1 May 1885 issue of the *Illustrated Naval and Military Magazine*:

> The term automatic has been applied to several forms of machine guns, in which all the functions of loading and firing are performed by operating a lever or crank. Strictly speaking, however, none of these are automatic guns, because the various functions are performed by machinery operated by hand. The Maxim gun, however, is really an automatic gun, and as far as is known, the first automatic ever made. All the functions of loading, cocking, firing, extracting the empty shells and expelling them from the gun, are performed by [the recoil] energy derived from the gun itself.

Since the invention of the handgun there has been a gradual development of the mechanical means to produce an ever-increasing volume of fire, delivered by, ideally, one man or two. An early device was the *orgue de bombarde* or organ gun, so called because the number of musket barrels resembled the pipes of an organ. Up to ten barrels were mounted side by side in a frame on a wheeled carriage; the barrels were so arranged that they could be fired singly, or by quick-match which ignited all the charges in the barrels in rapid succession. Organ guns were first used in the Battle of Piccardina, in 1467, when a Venetian general brought them into action with the cavalry of his vanguard. The Spanish commander, Pedro Navarro, employed organ guns against the French at Ravenna in 1512.

A great advance in design technology came with the patent granted to James Puckle of London in 1718, whose single-barrel revolver gun mounted on a tripod had at least the appearance of a machine gun.

Testing and timing the rate of fire of the Maxim in 1885. Hiram Maxim, the inventor, stands in the centre.

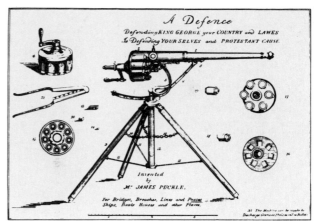

The hand-cranked machine gun patented by James Puckle in 1718.

He described his device as 'A Portable Gun or Machine called a Defence, that Discharges so often and so many Bullets, and can be so Quickly Loaded as renders it next to impossible to Carry any ship by Boarding.' The gun worked like this:

> It has a single barrel and a rotating chamber-piece, consisting of short cylinders fastened round a hollow centre, which works on a horizontal pin attached to the barrel. Several sets of chamber-pieces, each containing six or more chambers, may be used with the same barrel, so that as soon as all the charges of one set have been fired from one chamber-piece, it is un-screwed from the fixed pin or axis on which it revolves, and another chamber-piece, ready charged, is put in its place. The shapes of the chambers and of the bullets may be varied, some for shooting *square* bullets against Turks, others for shooting *round* bullets against Christians.

Puckle's gun was operated by hand crank and fired by flintlock. The *London Journal* of 31 March 1722 reported that the weapon could be fired by one man sixty-three times in seven minutes. Even so, naval and military authorities showed very little interest and Puckle's Machine Company failed. As a sceptical critic had predicted:

> A rare invention to destroy the crowd
> Of fools at home instead of foes abroad.
> Fear not my friends, this terrible machine;
> They're only wounded who have shares therein.

Further development of the machine gun proper had to wait the coming of the percussion system of igniting the charge, and the metallic cartridge.

Dragonship, a US helicopter gunship firing at ground target in Vietnam with Vulcan M61 electric-powered 20mm cannon operating on the Gatling multi-barrel principle. (Painting by Attilio Sinagra for the US Air Force Art Collection)

Scientific American

A WEEKLY JOURNAL OF PRACTICAL INFORMATION, ART, SCIENCE, MECHANICS, CHEMISTRY, AND MANUFACTURES.

Vol. XL.—No. 24.
[NEW SERIES.]

NEW YORK, JUNE 14, 1879.

[$3.20 per Annum.
[POSTAGE PREPAID.]

THE GATLING

The first practical machine gun was that invented in 1862 by Dr Richard J. Gatling of Chicago. In basic terms, it consisted of a number of rifle-barrels (usually ten) revolving in a circle around a fixed central axis. Behind each barrel was a bolt, complete with firing pin and spring and extractor. The metal cartridges were carried in a hopper or slide above the gun, and fell by their own weight in front of the open breech of each barrel as it came round. By turning the crank handle at the side of the gun, barrels and bolts were revolved, each barrel being fired in succession when it arrived at a certain point in its circuit.

The Gatling, in common with most machine guns, fired the standard military rifle cartridge, at rates from 200 to 600 rounds per minute; but because of constant jamming owing to the imperfect uniformity of cartridges of the time the average rate was some 280 shots per minute. The Gatling was adopted by the US military. Although little used in the Civil War, it saw wide service later.

Gatlings were used boldly and intelligently in the Spanish-American War of 1898. In the US assault on San Juan Hill in Cuba, Lieutenant John H. Parker was in command of the Gatling Gun Detachment. Parker believed that his guns, which normally played a defensive role in battle, could be of decisive importance in the attack by giving superiority of fire to the infantry (and dismounted cavalry) just when most needed. Receiving permission to advance his guns, Parker brought the detachment abreast of the infantry, and ahead of some elements, and opened fire. Theodore Roosevelt, who fought in the battle wrote in *The Rough Riders*:

> Suddenly, above the cracking of the carbines, rose a peculiar drumming sound, and some of the men cried, 'The Spanish machine guns!' Listening, I made out that it came from flat ground to the left, and jumped to my feet . . . shouting aloud with exultation, 'It's the Gatlings, men, our Gatlings!' Lieutenant Parker was bringing his four Gatlings into action, and shoving them nearer and nearer the front . . .

This, the US Army's first use of close-support machine guns in the attack, was decisive in the capture of San Juan Hill. Parker's initiative developed an important principle of fire and manoeuvre

The New Model Gatling Gun on the cover of the Scientific American *of 14 June 1879.*

(overleaf) *Lieutenant Parker and his Gatling Gun Detachment at San Juan Hill, Cuba, during the Spanish-American War of 1898.* (From the painting by H. Charles McBarron, courtesy of US Army)

– the use of close-support machine guns in the assault. Roosevelt was of the opinion that 'Parker deserved rather more credit than any other one man in the campaign,' because he proved by his own exertions that the machine gun 'could do invaluable work on the field of battle, as much in attack as in defence.'

Richard Gatling with his Bulldog Model of 1893.

MITRAILLEUSE

The first machine gun to be used in a European war was the Montigny Mitrailleuse, from the French *mitraille* meaning 'grapeshot'. It was invented in 1851 by a Belgian officer, Captain Fafschamps, and manufactured by the Belgian company of Montigny. The mitrailleuse consisted of thirty-seven rifle barrels fitted in an outer casing, the whole revolving round a common axis. The cartridges were carried in a perforated plate. To load the gun the plate was placed in grooves and locked in the breech, which was then forced home, each cartridge entering one of the chambers. The gun was operated by a crank handle which, when turned, revolved the barrels and fired each of the cartridges in succession. All thirty-seven barrels were discharged in one revolution.

The mitrailleuse had great potential if properly used, but it was badly deployed in the Franco-Prussian War of 1870–1. Adopted by the French Army and first issued in 1869, the mitrailleuse was regarded as a 'secret weapon' by the French, who placed enormous faith in the firepower of this infernal machine gun. Using the same rifle cartridge as the French infantry, with a range of 1,000yd, the mitrailleuse was expected to mow down the Prussians with impunity.

But the astute Prussians knew all about the machine gun, thanks to their master spy Wilhelm Steiber. Before the coming war broke out, Steiber and his assistants had spent eighteen months in France learning about the mitrailleuse and other military secrets and generally paving the way for a Prussian victory. The French military made the cardinal error of regarding the mitrailleuse as a form of artillery, mounted high on wheels and used in action as an adjunct to field guns, instead of forward close-support for the infantry.

Used at long range the mitrailleuse was worthless. When faced with the machine gun, unconcealed by trees or brush, the Prussians brought up a light fieldpiece to destroy the conspicuous weapon. On the few occasions, such as the Battle of Gravelotte, that the mitrailleuse guns were employed intelligently, under cover of trees in the infantry firing line, they proved effective.

The Montigny Mitrailleuse suffered the same malady of jamming as the Gatling: jams were frequent in non-automatic machine guns until the solid-drawn brass cartridge case had been perfected. The Gatling was introduced into the British Army in 1875 and saw service in India, Africa and Egypt. An incident in the Egyptian campaign inspired Sir Henry Newbolt's celebrated lines in *Vitai Lampada*:

The sand of the desert is sodden red –
Red with the wreck of a square that broke;
The Gatling's jammed and the Colonel dead,
And the regiment blind with dust and smoke . . .

Other machine guns used by British forces in this period were the Nordenfelt and the Gardner. The former, designed by a Swedish engineer named Palmcrantz, was manufactured by the Swedish Nordenfelt Guns and Ammunition Company. The Gardner was a product of an American officer of that name. Both guns were somewhat similar in design, with a row of rifle barrels fixed side by side (like the ancient organ gun). The cartridges were contained in a vertical magazine above the breech action, from which they fell by gravity into position in front of whichever breech was open, and were subsequently fired through the action of the lever handle closing the breech.

Russian Maxim-type gun of World War One. Note the typical Russian combined wheeled carriage and tripod.

The Montigny Mitrailleuse as used by the French in the Franco-Prussian War of 1870–1.

THE MAXIM GUN

When the automatic Maxim gun came on the scene in 1883, it rendered all mechanical machine guns obsolete. Sir Hiram Maxim (1840–1916), an American who became a naturalised British subject, was a born inventor. The scientific principle behind his gun was the use of recoil power (the energy given off by the cartridge gases) to fire the weapon continuously. Maxim got the idea to use the force of recoil when one day the heavy 'kick' of a high-calibre rifle he had fired bruised his shoulder. He decided to harness this hitherto wasted power to move the breech-bolt backward, thus extracting and ejecting the empty case. When the breech-bolt again moved forward, pushing a fresh case into the chamber, the gun was then cocked and ready to fire the next round. By keeping the trigger depressed the cycle of fire was continuous until stopped by either releasing the trigger or expending the belt of ammunition. To counter the great heat generated by continuous firing, Maxim surrounded the single barrel with a steel jacket containing cold water; the water was normally replaced every two thousand rounds.

The Maxim was a resounding international success, adopted by the armies of Great Britain, Germany, Russia and many other nations. It was

particularly effective against the mass onrushes of natives armed with spears and swords. As Hilaire Belloc succinctly put it: 'Whatever happens we have got, the Maxim gun, and they have not.' At the battle of Omdurman in the Sudan, on 2 September 1898, the Maxims of the British-Egyptian force were credited with inflicting fifteen thousand casualties on the Dervish army. Major von Tiedemann, a German observer, witnessed the Maxim gun battery in action:

The gunners did not get the range at once, but as soon as they found it the enemy went down in heaps, and it was evident that the six Maxim

The Maxim, a diagram published in the Illustrated War News *of 3 March 1915.*

guns were doing a large share of repelling the Dervish rush . . . [The Maxims] were firing .303 cartridges with smokeless powder, and besides their rapidity of fire, they had the advantage of longer range with a flatter trajectory than that of the Martini rifles, with which the Egyptian troops to right and left of them were armed.

The Russo-Japanese War

The first big conflict between major military powers in which machine guns were used extensively and with telling effect by both sides was the Russo-Japanese War of 1904–5, waged mainly in Manchuria. The Russians mostly used Maxims of .312in (7.92mm) calibre manufactured in Britain by Vickers Sons and Maxim. The Japanese had the French-produced Hotchkiss, manufactured under licence in Japan; this gun was gas operated and air cooled.

In the battle of Mukden, sixteen Russian Maxims – used eight at a time – repelled seven fierce enemy attacks. Each firing session lasted only a few minutes, and during that time, the eight guns not firing were being overhauled, cleaned and oiled. The sixteen guns fired a total two hundred thousand rounds and ended the day in excellent condition. German military observers were particularly impressed with machine gun firepower.

A German report summing up the lessons of the Russo-Japanese War included the following comments:

Machine guns were extraordinarily successful. In defence of entrenchments especially they had the most telling effect on the assailants at the moment of the assault. But they were also of service to the attack, being extremely useful in sweeping the crest of the enemy parapets . . . The

British Vickers machine gun in action during World War One. (From a painting by W. B. Wollen, 1915)

fire of six machine guns is equal to that of a battalion [of riflemen] . . . Whichever of the two opponents has at his disposal the larger number of machine guns, has thereby at his command such a *superiority of fire* that he is able to give an efficient support to his infantry. He can occupy a considerable front, with smaller groups of infantry – an economy in manpower. Infantry is thus more free to manoeuvre and becomes more mobile.

1914

The German military took the lessons to heart. The Kaiser was an enthusiast of the Maxim gun. By the time war broke out in Europe in 1914, the German armies had some fifty thousand machine guns of the Maxim type. But the British Expeditionary Force that landed in France, in August 1914, had a total of only 120 Vickers-Maxims at its disposal. When the Germans launched their mass infantry attacks on the outnumbered BEF at Mons on 23 August 1914 it was only the rapid and accurate rifle fire of highly trained British regulars that saved the day. Britain's army top brass had failed to grasp the growing significance of machine guns in modern warfare. 'It took our General Staff many months of terrible loss,' wrote David Lloyd George in his *War Memoirs*, 'to realise the worth of the machine gun.'

The Vickers .303in MG

The British firm of Vickers acquired Maxim's company and the rights to the gun. Vickers improved the weapon and in November 1912 the War Office accepted the Vickers gun Mark I .303in (7.7mm) calibre for general service. The Vickers Mk I and its variants saw wide service in both World War One and World War Two. A number of Vickers guns in .30in (7.62mm) calibre were manufactured by the Colt company in the United States during World War One for use by American forces.

British Vickers gun crew on the Somme in July 1916.

After serving the British 'Tommy' for fifty-six years, it was declared obsolete in 1968 by the Ministry of Defence. The Vickers went out fighting – it was used in action that year by the Parachute Regiment in the Middle East in the Radfan campaign.

GAS-OPERATED MACHINE GUNS

All automatic weapons work on basically the same principle. The expansion of gases has the effect of pushing back the cocking action as well as expelling the bullet, and some form of spring was responsible for the forward action by which the explosive was detonated. John Moses Browning (1855–1926) is a significant name in firearms history. This brilliant American gun designer invented a method of harnessing gas energy to perform the automatic stages of extracting, ejecting, feeding and firing cartridges. A small portion of the hot propellant gases was diverted via a hole near the muzzle inside the barrel's bore, into the auxiliary cylinder, forcing the piston backward, setting in motion the reloading mechanism. Browning's system, known as 'gas operated', gave rise to a new category of light machine guns and automatic weapons, a category which came to be essential to infantrymen.

The Lewis .303in Light Automatic

A notable gas-operated light machine gun (LMG) of World War One was that designed by the American Samuel Maclean and promoted by fellow American Colonel Lewis, after whom the gun was named. The Lewis gun had a cyclic rate of 600 rounds per minute, fed by a top-mounted circular magazine. A full magazine held forty-seven rounds and weighed 4.5lb; an empty one 1.5lb. With the .303in Lewis, the gas pressure was about 19 tons per square inch. This force was used to operate loading and also in cooling the barrel and the magazine. The Lewis could be fired from a bipod or from the hip. It was also modified for use by aircraft. The Lewis saw service in both world wars with US and British forces.

PATROL IN NO MAN'S LAND

World War One on the Western Front did not all devolve upon artillery bombardments of static trench lines and 'going over the top' to confront mass machine gun fire. There was a good deal of infantry work involved, consisting mainly of obtaining information about the enemy, and maintaining areas. These patrols relied upon the fieldcraft of the soldiers and the normal disciplined use of personal weapons and unit firepower application.

In all patrols men would always avoid skylines as this gave away their position immediately. Daylight patrols might be undertaken depending largely upon conditions in No Man's Land. Only a few men were generally required, moving by bounds from cover to cover. Initiative and prompt decision-making abilities were vital. Reliable, resourceful men were required. They would have knowledge of map-reading, compass work, aeroplane photographs, report-writing, use of ground and cover, use of the telescope and periscope, and patrolling and keeping touch. They also needed to be disciplined in combat and able to use their weapons to effect. Men going on patrol would carry their rifle and ammunition, and bombs and bayonet if required. The men would not wear their steel helmets, as they might make a noise.

There were three types of patrol: Defensive; Reconnaissance; and Fighting. A defensive or protective patrol consisted of one scout and two or three men. As a standing patrol, it was best used on a front where the line had sapheads. Tasked with watching and listening for enemy patrols, and protecting minefields and obstacles that could not be covered from the main line, its purpose was to keep the line more secure and give the troops more confidence.

A reconnaissance patrol generally consisted of a few men for scouting No Man's Land, but the size of the patrol depended on the area of ground, distance between the lines and enemy activity. Three men were generally found sufficient. The men were never to lose touch with each other, nor bunch together. A reconnaissance patrol might work in conjunction with a fighting patrol, going out in front to reconnoitre the ground and bring back information, so that the fighting patrol could be mounted to greater effect.

The size of a fighting patrol depended upon the ground, activities of the enemy and the distance between lines. A fighting patrol might be sent out to maintain security in an area by taking offensive action against enemy patrols. It could be sent out with a specific objective – for instance, to raid a troublesome machine gun nest – or to capture prisoners or equipment for intelligence purposes.

The enemy would also have his patrols out. Clashes in No Man's Land were not infrequent. The element of surprise played a big part in the success of a fighting patrol. It was important to have seasoned troops, for, when coming suddenly into contact with an enemy patrol, the patrol which recovered first generally got the better of the firefight.

Formation of fighting patrol, Western Front 1915-18

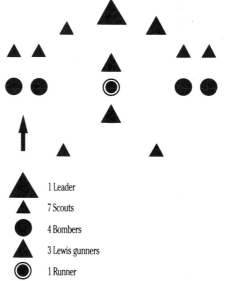

1 Leader
7 Scouts
4 Bombers
3 Lewis gunners
1 Runner

The patrol needed enough firepower to look after itself. The Lewis might be comparatively heavy, but automatic firepower was invaluable if contact was made with the enemy. Lewis guns could lay down covering fire to neutralise the enemy while the riflemen got into position to assault the enemy. If the patrol were attacking a position, it would carry a greater weight of automatic firepower, in order to cover the riflemen as they went in with bayonets fixed.

Today, the types of patrol remain the same. The principles do not differ, although the detail organisation, the equipment and the skills required do. The firepower, man for man, has increased alarmingly.

A Bren light machine gun in action during the Normandy campaign, 1944.

Australians firing a Lewis gun at Japanese aircraft during a low-flying raid on Darwin in1942.

A principal feature of the Lewis was that the rounds fired aided the cooling of the same barrel they helped to get so hot. The gases trapped in the gas port followed the bullet out of the barrel and provided the force by which the bullet was pushed forward. When the gases reached the barrel mouthpiece, they expanded into a fan shape and struck the forepart of the aluminium radiator-casing around the barrel, thereby expelling all the air so that a vacuum was created. This caused a continuous stream of cool air through the fins of the radiator, passing from the rear to the front. The air entered the cooling system at the point where it was most needed – the rear of the barrel, and passed forward to the muzzle where it was needed least.

There were several features which made the .303 Lewis such an effective infantry weapon. Weighing barely 27lb, it was easy to carry. It was compact, offering a small target to an enemy. It required only a firer and a loader to operate it, but its firing capacity was equal to at least fifty riflemen. It offered rapid gun-laying – fifty riflemen shifting to an alternative target would have made considerable movement, and could not have moved so quickly. Its 600 round per minute rate of fire, combined with a muzzle velocity of 2,460ft per second and 1,900yd range, had a paralysing effect on the enemy. Used intelligently, the opposition could be wiped out before they got the chance to reply.

Professional Lewis gunners developed 'eyes at their fingertips', through constant stripping of the gun, handling and naming its components, and knowing by touch every part of the weapon until they could strip and name all components automatically, even when blindfolded.

The fact that a machine gun was capable of sustained fire of 600 rounds per minute, does not mean that to be effective an entire magazine should be emptied in one long burst. In fact, the British Army in World War Two officially counselled:

. . . the .303 Lewis should be fired in bursts of four or five rounds at the most and never until the target was sufficiently large and vulnerable. By using it haphazardly, its position would be disclosed to the enemy and its effectiveness destroyed.

The Bren Light Machine Gun

In the British Army, the Lewis was superseded in 1938 by an LMG of Czech origin. Designed and developed in Czechoslovakia at Brno, the British adapted the gun at Enfield to fire the standard British .303in (7.7mm) round. It was named the Bren, from BRno and ENfield. It served the British and Commonwealth forces, and the forces of other nations, for more than forty years.

Gas operated, the Bren had a cyclic rate of 480 rounds per minute, normally fed by a distinctive vertically curved magazine holding thirty rounds. Single shots could also be fired. A spare barrel was carried into action and changed after firing ten magazines. This was a simple operation: the forepart of the barrel was grasped in one hand, given a half-turn and pulled out, the new barrel being fitted by reversing the method. The long-serving Bren was an LMG par excellence. Renowned for its accuracy (there was very little vibration) and reliability, it was trusted and respected by all those whose lives depended upon its performance. It could be fired on a bipod or a tripod, or from the hip in the assault role.

The Bren featured in many heroic Victoria Cross winning actions. In August 1942, Private Bruce Kingsbury of the 2/14th Battalion Australian Military Forces was serving in New Guinea. The battalion was in action when a savage Japanese attack broke through the battalion's right flank and created a critical situation. Kingsbury, on his own initiative, charged into the breach. Firing his Bren from the hip in controlled bursts, he inflicted heavy casualties on the Japanese before he was killed. His bravery saved the position from being overrun. He was awarded Britain's highest decoration for gallantry in battle.

An air-cooled weapon capable of a high rate of fire (automatic or single rounds), the Bren was fired shoulder-controlled either from a bipod or from a tripod. The chief characteristic was its power of delivering a volume of fire with the employment of few men. When fired from the bipod, the effective range was 1,000yd. When fired from the tripod, given perfect conditions of visibility, this distance could be increased. To avoid overheating, strain and excessive expenditure of ammunition and, at the same time, to produce the necessary volume of fire whilst maintaining accuracy, it was best to fire in bursts of four or five rounds. The accuracy of the gun allowed only a small margin of error in aiming, range estimation or wind. Accurate observation of fire was therefore essential; if less than four or five rounds were fired in a burst, observation would be possible only in the most favourable circumstances. When the target allowed, single-shot firing should be used also to conserve ammunition. By means of single shots, very accurate shooting was possible.

Every man in a section had to be an efficient shot

SAS JEEP ATTACK

Machine guns were used with devastating effect by the British desert raiders of World War Two, the Special Air Service (SAS), founded by Major David Stirling. The SAS wrecked nearly four hundred enemy aircraft during the desert campaigns. A typical exploit was the attack on the German airfield at Sidi Haneish in July 1942.

Late one afternoon that July, Stirling returned from Cairo to his men who had endured eight days in caves in the middle of the desert behind enemy lines. Stirling had with him twenty brand new jeeps. Each jeep carried two pairs of Vickers 'K' guns, one forward pair beside the driver, and one pair at the back.

He also had an operation in mind. A few hours later, he outlined the plan. One of the aerodromes in the Fuka area, Sidi Haneish, known as Landing Ground 12, was serving as the Germans' principal staging area for all aircraft going to or coming from the front.

Stirling proposed to attack the landing ground and destroy every aircraft on it. The method of attack was novel – machine gun-armed jeeps, and the attack would be made at full moon, when the Germans would least expect an attack. They would have a forty-mile desert journey to make, and would have to escape in small parties as best they could after the attack.

That night, when it was dark, the SAS rehearsed the formations they would use for the attack. The eighteen jeeps would advance on the airfield in line abreast at five-yard intervals – that way, they could bring to bear upon the airfield's defences sixty-eight machine guns (the navigator's jeep would not be in the firing line). Stirling would fire a green Verey light and they would form two parallel columns of seven jeeps, with Stirling in the lead, two jeeps tucked close in beside his, and Sadler, the navigator, following. The formations were important: the line abreast gave the maximum frontal fire on their entry to the airfield; the two columns gave maximum fire down the flanks, both defensive and offensive when they would sweep down between the rows of aircraft.

They set out the next night after dark. A mile from Sidi Haneish, the jeeps formed up in line abreast, and began to roll, keeping tight formation. Half a mile from Sidi Haneish, the airfield suddenly lit up – a bomber was coming in to land. Stirling's gunners opened fire – the other thirty-two gunners followed. Tracer arced onto the airfield. Sixty-eight guns, each firing at 20 rounds per second. The airfield lights went out, and all plunged into darkness . . .

Stirling fired the green Verey two minutes later. The jeeps formed up in their parallel lines. The aircraft were lined up in rows on either side of the tarmac taxi-ways, like an air show. The jeeps made a circle of the airfield. The aircraft seemed to absorb bullets before suddenly fire broke out and their fuel caught light.

The Germans reacted slowly . . . but accurately. A mortar lobbed its shell between the two lines of jeeps. A heavy machine gun opened up. Stirling's jeep was lanced by a mortar shell splinter, and stopped. He changed jeeps. The machine gun was using tracer which simply advertised its exact position . . . it was quickly silenced.

Stirling ordered all guns to stop and all engines to be switched off. Surrounded by burning and exploding aircraft, with German troops rushing into defensive positions, the commander asked how much ammunition was left.

There was enough to carry on towards the Ju 52s they could make out on the perimeter of the landing ground. They started up and headed for them. Their Vickers made short work of them.

The jeeps then headed for the desert. Briefly, they gathered together and assessed their work. Six jeeps had been hit but were running; three had been knocked out. One gunner was dead. Flames colouring the desert sky marked the position of Sidi Haneish. The small group had destroyed twenty-five aircraft and damaged a further dozen.

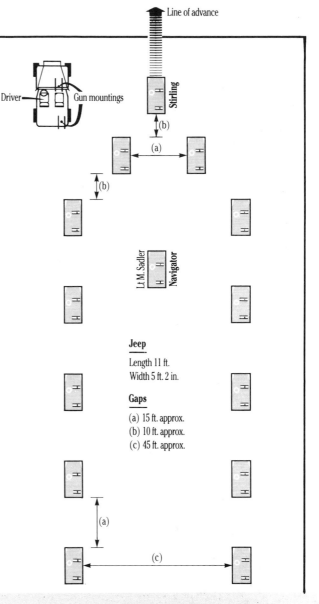

Driver — Gun mountings

Line of advance

Stirling

Lt M. Sadler

Navigator

Jeep

Length 11 ft.
Width 5 ft. 2 in.

Gaps

(a) 15 ft. approx.
(b) 10 ft. approx.
(c) 45 ft. approx.

British SAS jeep of World War Two equipped for desert raiding with a front-mounted US M2 Browning heavy machine gun. At the rear a pair of Vickers 'K' type designed for use against aircraft.

THE GENERAL PURPOSE MACHINE

GENERAL VIEW

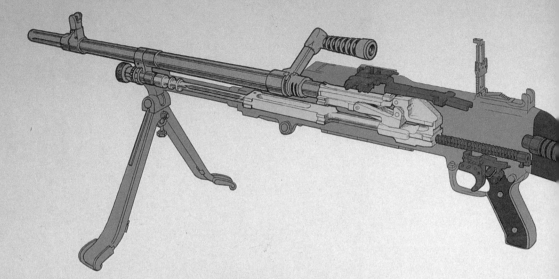

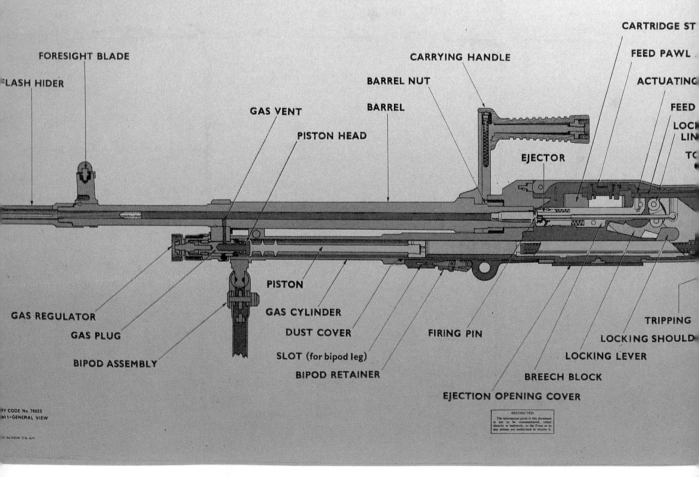

FORESIGHT BLADE

FLASH HIDER

GAS VENT

PISTON HEAD

CARRYING HANDLE

BARREL NUT

BARREL

CARTRIDGE ST

FEED PAWL

ACTUATING

FEED

LOC
LIN

T

EJECTOR

GAS REGULATOR

GAS PLUG

BIPOD ASSEMBLY

PISTON

GAS CYLINDER

DUST COVER

SLOT (for bipod leg)

BIPOD RETAINER

FIRING PIN

TRIPPING

LOCKING SHOULD

LOCKING LEVER

BREECH BLOCK

EJECTION OPENING COVER

EJECTOR

RY CODE No. 70025

m11-GENERAL VIEW

04/03/00 7(10) 60/9

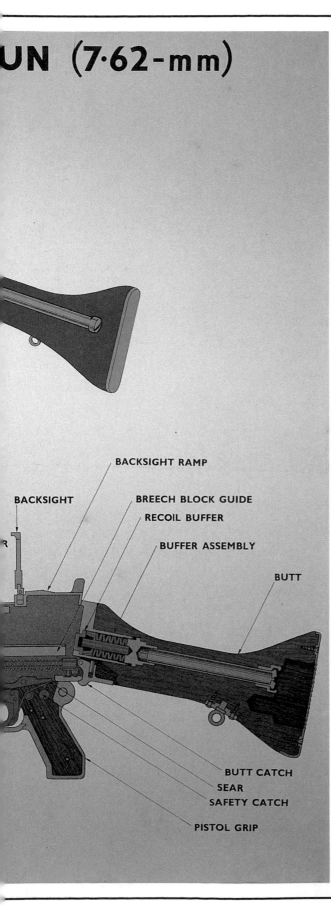

UN (7·62-mm)

BACKSIGHT

BACKSIGHT RAMP

BREECH BLOCK GUIDE

RECOIL BUFFER

BUFFER ASSEMBLY

BUTT

BUTT CATCH

SEAR

SAFETY CATCH

PISTOL GRIP

with the LMG, and in addition, be able to carry out every duty that would maintain the gun in action under all conditions. All men were interchangeable so far as LMG duties were concerned. All were able to carry the gun and get it quickly into action on any type of ground, to prepare it for firing and maintain it in action, to fire accurately at various rates according to the requirements of various types of targets, to observe and correct fire, and to assist forward movement by fire while, at the same time, ensuring that such fire did not endanger friendly troops. All men had to be able to fire with effect at low-flying aircraft.

Vickers 'K' (VGO)
In 1933, the Vickers-Berthier .303in gas-operated machine gun was adopted by the Indian Government as standard equipment for the Indian Army. It replaced the Hotchkiss and Lewis. Had not the Bren appeared, it was likely that the British Army also would have adopted it. Easy to carry, operate and strip, it was a reliable weapon.

In 1935, Vickers developed from the Vickers-Berthier an aircraft gun, designated Vickers Gas Operated but generally known as the Vickers 'K'. It was used as an observer's gun by the Royal Air Force. It could spit out 1,050 rounds per minute. From 1941, superseded by power-operated aircraft turrets, RAF stocks of the 'K' were offered to the army. They made up for a shortage of Brens. They were rugged, reliable weapons, and their high rate of fire was ideal for 'hit and run' work such as the Special Air Service undertook. It was often used against low-flying aircraft.

THE GPMG

The veteran Bren and the venerable Vickers eventually gave way to the ubiquitous General Purpose Machine Gun (GPMG) of today, a gun 'for all seasons' that can be fired from a bipod in the LMG's roles or from a tripod for sustained fire. The GPMG concept was pioneered and perfected by the Germans. The Maschinengewehr 1934, commonly abbreviated to MG34, was the first true GPMG, a creation of German ingenuity between the world wars when Germany was restricted from making heavy machine guns.

The MG34 in 7.92mm (.312in) calibre had a cyclic rate of 900 rounds per minute, could fire single shot or full automatic, and required a barrel change after every 250 rounds. Issued to the pre-war German Army, it equipped the Third Reich's forces and allies throughout World War Two. It served as the basic infantry section LMG, bipod-mounted, or on a tripod for sustained fire; it was used in an anti-aircraft role

British Army instruction chart on the General Purpose Machine Gun (GPMG).

and was mounted on various vehicles, including tanks.

The MG34 was a versatile and well-made weapon – too well made for quick, simple, mass production. Its successor was the durable MG42, a cheaper, tougher, speedily manufactured product using a maximum of steel stampings. It proved an excellent GPMG. About seven hundred and fifty thousand were produced between 1942 and the end of World War Two. So sound in design was the MG42 that when the new army of West Germany was formed in 1956, production of this notable GPMG was resumed to arm the Bundeswehr (Federal Defence Force). It was modified slightly to fire 7.62mm (.30in) NATO rounds and was redesignated MG2. The final version was the MG3.

INFANTRY ANTI-AIRCRAFT LMGs

Before the appearance of short-range battlefield anti-aircraft missiles, the LMG was the chief infantry anti-aircraft weapon. Experience had shown that where all-round defence was required, it was essential that the weapons should move round the man as with the hosepipe method, and not the man round the weapon as was the case with the anti-aircraft Bren LMG mounting (which resulted in the eventual abolition of the AA leg from the Bren LMG tripod). The hosepipe

method has the further advantage that any protective trench or weapon pit required, can be of much smaller dimensions than that required to take the firer and AA LMG mounting.

Low-level or dive-bombing air attacks within 2,000ft or 600yd (ground range) may be made at high speed and will be quickly over, allowing only three to four seconds during which effective fire is possible. These attacks may be repeated at frequent intervals, and be made either individually by aircraft flying along a column and diving in quick succession, or by a simultaneous converging attack by several aircraft from different directions. The dive bomber peels off at altitudes out of small arms range and dives on its target at an angle of approximately 80 degrees; after release of its bomb, it flattens out generally within range of small arms fire, and then either flies away close to the ground or climbs rapidly out of range.

Against undisciplined or demoralised troops, air attacks may have a decisive effect. It is of the utmost importance therefore that all ranks should be trained to withstand the noise of air attack and should be imbued with the necessity of hitting back as hard as possible. In this way very considerable damage can be done to enemy aircraft making such attacks too costly for him, and in addition ensuring that the morale of troops is kept up. Troops must not expect that the

After landing, German paratroops of World War Two quickly set up an MG34 ready for action.

Loading the MG34 with belt ammunition.

Another view of the MG34 that served as the basic infantry section light machine gun.

German troops of World War Two in action with MG34s.

aircraft when hit will crash immediately. If it remains in the air for only thirty seconds it will fly two or three miles. Personnel therefore must not lose heart if the accuracy of their fire does not bring immediate results.

Of utmost importance is a system whereby warning of the approach of hostile aircraft can be conveyed to troops. The maximum fire of all available small arms weapons should immediately be brought to bear on the attacking aircraft, unless, for purposes of concealment, specific orders to hold fire have been issued previously. To be effective, fire must be controlled. Speed in opening fire is essential. This requires strict fire discipline training as well as early recognition. When troops were on foot, the fire of all available LMGs and rifles would be used. In bivouacs, billets, or when otherwise halted, LMGs, suitably sited and concealed, should form the main small arms defence. Concealment from view was of prime importance, and a 360 degree arc of fire may have to be sacrificed in favour of concealment.

On the move, irrespective of light anti-aircraft protection, columns must be protected by LMGs mounted on Motely and other mountings moving within the column itself. No matter to what extent dispersion has taken place fire must always be controlled, and under no circumstances must it be allowed to become indiscriminate.

Sub-units whose primary role was anti-aircraft defence, such as the AA platoon of infantry battalions, were equipped with a special sight for engaging aircraft. It was not practicable to provide the ordinary man in the ranks with any form of anti-aircraft sight or other mechanical aid for either the rifle or the LMG. Their estimation of range can be limited to a knowledge of when fire can be usefully opened. Extreme accuracy of fire must, therefore, give way to quick retaliation, speed in opening fire, strict fire discipline and achieving the maximum volume of controlled fire.

The Heckler & Koch HK21E Light Machine Gun with tripod. It is capable of single shot, three-round burst, or continuous fire at 800 rounds per minute.

A Royal Marine Commando of 40 Cdo armed with the 7.62mm calibre GPMG.

9
THOMPSON GUNS
AND TERRORISTS

It was the morning of 14 February 1929, St Valentine's Day. On North Clark Street, Chicago, a black Cadillac pulled up outside a garage. Five men alighted. Three of them wore police uniforms. A number of passers-by saw all five go inside the dark garage building. Moments later, the passers-by heard what one described as the sound of a pneumatic drill. When the 'police party' drove away, they left behind in the garage seven bullet-riddled bodies. Al Capone's button men had just committed the infamous 'St Valentine's Day Massacre'.

But they missed their primary target – rival gang leader George 'Bugs' Moran, who arrived at the meeting in the garage late, narrowly escaping the fate of his men. In their guise as 'cops', Capone's gunmen had persuaded the rival mobsters to line up facing a brick wall. Then they cut them down with long, traversing bursts from two Thompson submachine guns.

THE SUBMACHINE GUN

The submachine gun, like the stylised urban American gangster, was a product of the twentieth century, and the Thompson, much used by gangsters and law officers in the 1920s and 1930s, became the symbol of gangsterism. Regular appearances in Hollywood's crime movies made the 'tommy gun' the most readily identified firearm of its period.

The submachine gun (SMG) or – in British World War Two parlance – the machine carbine, first appeared in the latter part of World War One. Conceived and developed as a light, hand-held, one-man weapon for close-quarter combat, firing standard issue pistol ammunition in the full automatic or semi-automatic mode, most SMGs operate on the 'blowback' or 'delayed blowback' self-loading principle.

The submachine gun is an automatic weapon operated by blowback action which can be fired in

The gangster victims of the St Valentine's Day Massacre in Chicago, 14 February 1929

single rounds or bursts. It is a short range weapon used to engage enemy at ranges up to 100yd. At greater distances the penetrative power of the bullet is considerably reduced. It is an ideal weapon for street-fighting, wood-clearing, or patrols – conditions when the enemy may appear suddenly at close range and in different directions, and can be attacked immediately either by fire from the shoulder without using the sights or fire from the waist.

Normally, submachine guns would be fired in bursts, and in the field, would be set at 'Automatic'. Bursts would rarely be more than two or three rounds. There are occasions, however, when single rounds, fired from the shoulder, are sufficient to deal with the enemy. But wielding the gun in gangster fashion was not the reality of war: soldiers used the gun intelligently.

One of the first SMGs proper, hand-held and operated by one man, was the German Bergmann Muskete of 1918, designed by Hugo Schmeisser for the Theodor Bergmann company and termed officially the Maschinen Pistole 18 (MP18). It fired the 9mm (.354in) Parabellum cartridge, the standard German pistol ammunition of the time. The magazine held thirty-two rounds. The Bergmann was issued to frontline stormtroopers in the final stages of the war. At about the same time, the Italian 9mm (.35in) Beretta Model 18, derived from the Villar Perosa light machine gun, was issued to the Arditi troops in the last months of the fighting.

The Thompson Gun

The Thompson gun missed World War One. Co-designed and promoted by Brigadier-General John T. Thompson (1860–1940), sometime member of the US Ordnance Department, the Thompson gun was conceived as an automatic rifle in about 1916–17. But the influence of co-designer, T. Eickhoff, led to the development of a hand-held machine gun to fire the US Army's .45in (11.43mm) pistol cartridge. Thompson formed a company, the Auto-Ordnance Corporation, to produce and market the weapons, the first of which were manufactured by the Colt Company.

The first production Thompson, the Model 1921, had a cyclic rate of 800 rounds per minute and the characteristic style of finned barrel (a cooling device) and front and rear vertical pistol grips with finger grooves. The journal *Scientific American* reported its deadly virtues:

> With its small size, its light weight, its tremendous rate of fire, and its ease of control, the Thompson Gun is probably the most efficient man killer of any firearms yet produced.

The Auto-Ordnance Corporation advertised their product as 'an ideal arm for the police', and firmly, if naively, stated that:

> Thompson Guns are for use by those on the side of law and order and Auto-Ordnance Corporation agents and dealers are authorized to make sales to responsible parties only.

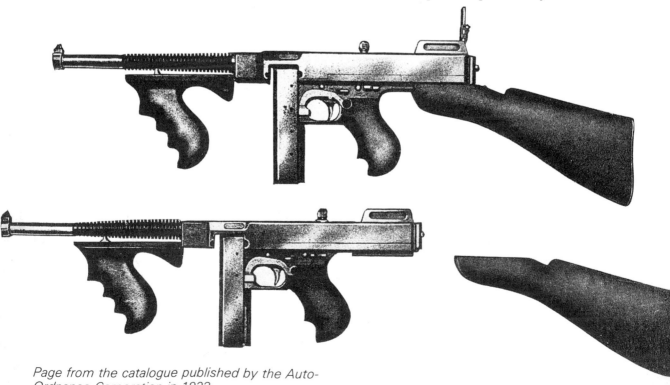

Page from the catalogue published by the Auto-Ordnance Corporation in 1923.

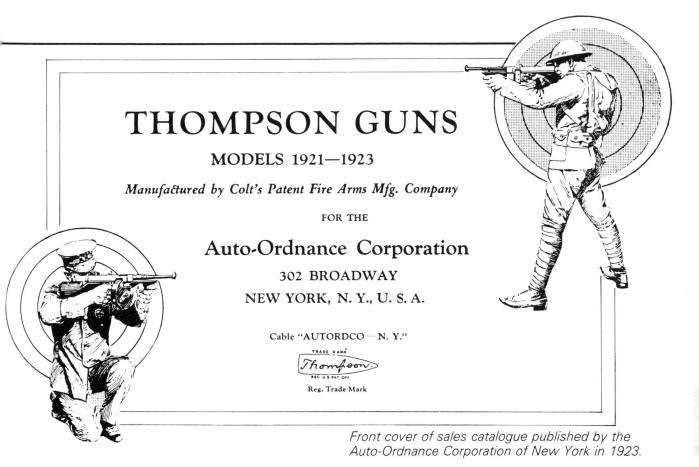

THOMPSON GUNS

MODELS 1921—1923

Manufactured by Colt's Patent Fire Arms Mfg. Company

FOR THE

Auto-Ordnance Corporation

302 BROADWAY

NEW YORK, N. Y., U. S. A.

Cable "AUTORDCO— N. Y."

TRADE MARK

Thompson

REC US PAT OFF

Reg. Trade Mark

Front cover of sales catalogue published by the Auto-Ordnance Corporation of New York in 1923.

An FBI agent firing a Thompson gun fitted with a Cutts Compensator at the muzzle, which reduced barrel climb. Note the ejected empty cases spinning in the air.

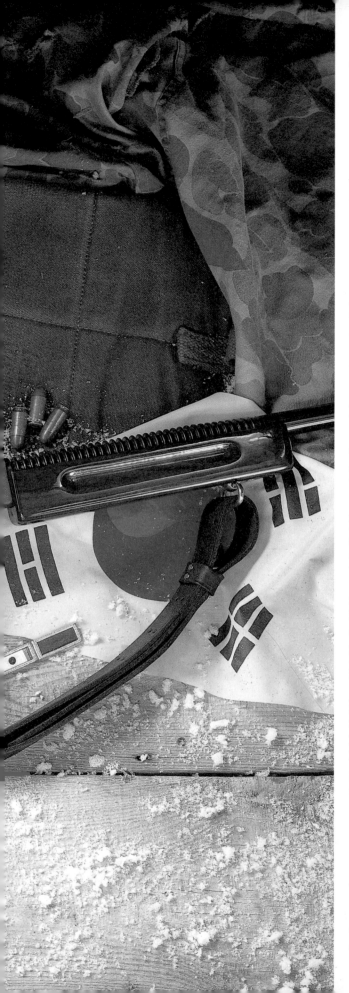

Gangsters, of course, obtained as many 'tommy guns' as they needed through underworld armourers, or, like John Dillinger, by raiding police and military arsenals. General Thompson never ceased to be appalled by the fact that his gun had fallen into criminal hands and had gained such notoriety. A crime reporter on *Collier's* magazine described the advent of the Thompson gun as 'the greatest aid to bigger and better business the criminal has discovered in this generation', then went on to call the gun a 'diabolical machine of death'.

Perhaps the first mobster to use the Thompson was Frank McErland, who headed a Chicago gang, in an attempt to kill rival gang chief Spike O'Donnell in September 1925. Lacking practice with the new weapon, McErland missed with every shot! With its high cyclic rate and resultant excessive muzzle climb, the 'burp gun' was not an accurate weapon until the Cutts Compensator was fitted in 1926. Designed by Colonel Cutts of the US Marine Corps, his device is a short, top-slotted tube fixed to the muzzle that directs escaping gas upwards, thus forcing the muzzle down, permitting accurate burst firing and reducing recoil.

The first 'tommy gun' killing of a New York gangster was that of Frankie Yale, in July 1927. He was riddled with bullets in his car, by underworld enemies. Gunmen who allegedly excelled in the use of the weapon were dubbed 'Machine Gun' Kelly and 'Machine Gun' Jack McGurn. It is believed that McGurn was actively involved in the St Valentine's Day Massacre. When the law investigated the massacre, a pioneer in firearms identification, Colonel Calvin Goddard, was brought in to give evidence to the coroner's jury. He identified the seventy empty .45in cartridge cases at the scene as having been fired from two Thompsons, one with a fifty-round drum magazine, the other with a twenty-round box magazine. Goddard later matched the cases and bullets to a brace of Thompsons abandoned in a hide-out used by freelance assassin Fred 'Killer' Burke, but he was never brought to trial for the crime.

The 1921 Thompson underwent a number of modifications over the years. The gun reached a highpoint with the Model 1928, which was adopted by the US Navy and Army. It had a cyclic rate of 600 rounds per minute. In the Nicaraguan campaign of the mid-1920s against the guerrilla leader Augusto Sandino, the US Marine Corps used the Thompson gun in jungle combat, which often involved firefights at ranges of 50ft or less. The Thompson was ideal in these conditions.

Sparkling special edition Korean War Commemorative Thompson issued by The American Historical Foundation of Richmond, Virginia. The trigger, front and rear sights, Cutts Compensator, swivel mounts and activator knob are gold plated.

A member of the German paramilitary Green Police of the 1920s, holding a Bergmann MP1918.

Finely made and expensive to manufacture, the 1923 model, complete with twenty-round box magazine, retailed at US $175. A fifty-round drum magazine cost US $21. When America entered World War Two, in 1941, the Thompson was greatly simplified for mass production and designated for government use as the SMG M1 and later M1A1.

The Thompson, in its mixed variants, was much favoured by special forces in World War Two, such as the US Rangers and paratroops, and Allied commando units. The Thompson entered heraldic history by being incorporated into the badge of the British Combined Operations Command – a mark of distinction indeed. Over two million Thompsons have been produced to date. Today, the Auto-Ordnance Corporation of West Hurley, New York, still manufacture Thompson guns in the classic configurations.

In the US Army, the Thompson Sub-Machine Gun M1 began to replace all earlier models and types from around 1944. It differed from the earlier types in several respects, the most important being that the fixed backsight consisted of an aperture and a 'U' sight; the butt could not be detached from the pistol grip; there was no 'H' piece or felt pads incorporated; the cocking handle was similar to that of the Sten and fitted into the right side of the bolt; and the buffer was not integral with the buffer rod which considerably simplified stripping.

To fill a Thompson's magazine, hold the magazine in the left hand, ribs away from the body. Pick up a convenient number of rounds in the right hand and ensure that they are clean. Place each round in the top of the magazine, base first; then press it downwards and backwards into place. Count the number of rounds. The magazine holds twenty rounds. To empty it, press each round forward with the nose of a bullet, or remove with finger and thumb.

To load the Thompson, hold it with the right hand on the pistol grip, forefinger outside the trigger guard, butt under the arm, and barrel point to the front and downwards. Turn the Thompson to the right, take the magazine in the left hand, ribs to the rear, and insert it in the recess in front of the trigger guard. Push the magazine in and ensure that it is fully home.

The change lever, positioned just above and behind the trigger on the left, controlled automatic or single-round firing. If it were pushed forward, the Thompson fired bursts; if backwards, single rounds. The lever could be moved backward only when the action was cocked.

To fire it, the gunner pulled the weapon close into his left side, the butt under the arm, grasped the pistol grip with his right hand then pulled back the cocking handle, grasped the foregrip with his left hand, put his right forefinger on the trigger and squeezed . . .

Some Thompsons had a fixed aperture backsight for ranges up to 100yd; in this case, the rule for aiming was the same as for a light machine gun.

Others had an adjustable tangent backsight which was unnecessary, and instead the V-shaped recess in the cocking handle was used. The rule for aiming was therefore the same as for a rifle.

In the US Army, the handsome but heavy Thompson was replaced as the standard SMG by the cheap, ugly, lightweight but practical and robust M3. Known to GIs as the 'grease gun' from its plain, functional shape, the M3 first appeared in December 1942. A product of US Ordnance, the M3 was influenced in design and mass manufacture by the German MP40 and the British Sten.

The German MP38 and MP40

In the development of the SMG, the German MP38 must be regarded as seminal in design and construction. When the German Army in 1938 decided to adopt an SMG in large numbers, the Erfurt firm of Erma-Werke produced the MP38 in 9mm (.354in) Parabellum pistol calibre, using a magazine holding thirty-two rounds at a cyclic rate of 500 rounds per minute. The weapon was innovative in that it was the first to be made of metal and plastic only, the first to have a folding steel butt or stock, and the first to be constructed of stamped steel components.

A main fault of the MP38 was its primitive safety device: if the gun was accidentally dropped or knocked, it could fire off a round. This weakness, and other minor faults, were rectified in the improved MP40, which used even more stamped and pressed steel components for cheap mass production – the unit cost was sixty Reichmarks, equal to about US $22. Over a million MP38s and MP40s were manufactured during World War Two. The archetypal German SMG is often referred to as the 'Schmeisser', although this is profoundly misleading as Hugo Schmeisser had no part in its design; ironically, the gun he *did* design, the original MP18 of late World War One, is known as the Bergmann. The MP40 was a much-prized Allied war trophy, and Soviet soldiers used many of these captured weapons against the Nazi invaders.

The Soviet PPSh1941

The most ubiquitous Russian SMG of World War Two was the PPSh1941. Designed by Georgi Shpagin, the PP indicated 'Pistolet Pulemet', or machine pistol, and the 'Sh' stood for Shpagin. Operated by simple blowback, it fired the standard Soviet 7.62mm (.300in) Tokarev pistol cartridge, fed by a drum holding seventy-one rounds or by a box magazine holding thirty-five rounds.

A cheaper replacement for the PPD 38/40 designed by Degtyarev, the PPSh1941 had no parts that required expensive machining and hand-finishing, and used stamped steel and welded components which could be manufactured with minimum factory tooling. The PPSh's distinctive perforated barrel jacket extended past the muzzle mouth to act as a primitive compensator to reduce muzzle-climb when fired automatically. The Soviet Union manufactured some five million of this successful weapon.

Russian soldiers on reconnaissance in World War Two. One carries a captured German MP38/40.

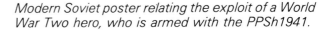

The MP38/40, the archetypal German SMG, is often wrongly referred to as the 'Schmeisser'. (Illustration from *Signal* the German propaganda magazine)

Modern Soviet poster relating the exploit of a World War Two hero, who is armed with the PPSh1941.

The Sten Gun

Great Britain was a late starter in original SMG design. The British Army had again failed to take proper note of recent warfare, notably the use of Spanish-manufactured blowback SMGs in the Spanish Civil War. When World War Two broke out in 1939, Britain purchased large numbers of the US Thompson gun but found it too expensive to buy or to manufacture. With the German Wehrmacht poised to invade, what was required urgently was a cheap, simple product, home-designed and made: enter the Sten machine carbine, surely the cheapest and ugliest of all SMGs. The Sten progressed through a series of improved marks. Over four million Stens were produced and it remained in service with the British Army until the 1960s.

Designed and developed at the Royal Small Arms Factory at Enfield by Major Sheppard and Mr Turpin, the Sten derived its name from their initials and ENfield. For rapidity and simplicity, the system of sub-component manufacture and the simple horizontal box magazine were copied from the MP40. The Sten would fire most makes of 9mm ammunition, including German and Italian. It had a cyclic rate of 50 rounds per minute. Thirty-two rounds were contained in a magazine. The Sten's magazine spring was too powerful to enable filling to be done quickly by hand; a filler was used, most commonly the Mark IV filler.

Stamped out and welded up, the Sten was as basic as possible, mass-produced as a dispensable weapon intended for hard and extensive use. When it broke down or wore out, it was dumped and replaced. It cost about £2 10s to manufacture. The Sten Mark I entered service with British troops in the summer of 1941. The Mark I had a fixed barrel with a full length casing, perforated and fitted with sloping swivel, flash eliminator, and foresight protectors. It had a wooden fore-end with folding forward hand grip, and a skeleton butt, and a fixed magazine housing.

It was fitted with a fixed aperture backsight for ranges up to 100yd; the rule for aiming was as for the LMG. The type of fire was altered by moving the stud on the trigger mechanism casing. By pressing in the side marked 'R' (round), the Sten fired single rounds; if the side marked 'A' (automatic), bursts. To fire it, the gunner thrust the butt into his left shoulder, grasped the pistol grip with his right hand, released the cocking handle from the safety slot, grasped the barrel nut with the left hand well clear of the ejection opening and the wrist under the magazine, put his right forefinger on the trigger . . . and squeezed.

The British Sten gun, cheap and simple to mass produce. Over four million were churned out during World War Two.

Russians in a village near Kharkov armed with the PPSh1941 submachine gun and, bottom, the Degtyarev light machine gun.

The Mark II had no woodwork, a removable barrel with no flash eliminator, a tubular butt and a foresight at the fore-end of the breech casing. The Mark II was a simpler version of the Mark I: easy to manufacture, and to strip and clean in the field, it could be quickly dismantled for concealment. More than two million Sten Mark IIs were produced, of which many were air-dropped to partisan and guerrilla groups all over Europe. Some resistance movements produced their own copies of the Sten in underground workshops. Even the Germans were impressed by the gun's skeletal simplicity and in 1944 the firm of Mauser turned out twenty-five thousand exact copies of the Mark II.

The Mark III had a breech-casing continued forward to form barrel casing with a rib running full length along the top; and a foresight, with no protector, at muzzle end. The Mark IV's trigger mechanism casing was not fixed by screws but sprung on. It had a Mark II type of butt. The Mark V was as the Mark II with wooden butt and pistol grips, Mark IV cocking handle, and a foresight with protector as for the No 4 rifle. It took the bayonet for the No 4 rifle. Its pistol grips were removable by an armourer. A plate was provided to enable it to be fired without the butt. There was a butt trap for an oil bottle and pull-through.

The Sterling
The Sten was superseded in 1953 by the 9mm (.354in) Sterling. Fed by a thirty-two-round magazine, it can fire single shots or bursts. It was developed and manufactured by Sterling Engineering from a design by George W. Patchett who, in June 1966, was awarded £116,000 by a High Court judge as payment in lieu of royalties for British Government use of his gun.

During the Borneo jungle campaign of 1962–6, the silenced version was used by SAS patrols to ambush Indonesian troops at track and river crossings. In the British Army L2A3 version, the Sterling was used during the Falklands War of 1982.

Heckler & Koch MPs
The West German firm of Heckler & Koch GmbH, situated at Oberndorf-Neckar was formed in 1949 by three engineers, Messrs Heckler, Koch and Seidel. Heckler & Koch (HK) produce a notable series of innovative automatic firearms including rifles, SMGs and pistols.

The British SAS is a regiment with a policy of using the best equipment available, home-produced or foreign, and accordingly replaced the American-made Ingram MAC10 in their armoury with the HK MP5. Although the 9mm Ingram was very small and light and could fire more than 1,000 rounds per minute, it tended to spray bullets over too wide an area with the danger that innocent people as well as terrorists could get killed, whereas the HK MP5 was noted for its accuracy.

The MP5 series of seven variants – which differ in fixed or retractable butt stocks, sights, and ultra-short design – fire 9mm (.354in) ammunition in single shots or bursts, fed from a fifteen- or thirty-round magazine. The MP5 is recoil-operated, with stationary barrel and delayed roller locked bolt system. Its high accuracy in the single-fire mode, and its safety, result from the fact that it fires from the closed bolt

The Heckler & Koch MP5KA1, ultra-short (325mm) design specially suited for carrying concealed.

TRUCK BOMB TERROR

In October 1983 a fanatical Moslem terrorist drove a truckload of high explosive into the HQ of the US Marine Corps battalion stationed in Beirut on a peace-keeping mission. The truck smashed through the perimeter fence and penetrated the entrance lobby before the kamikaze driver detonated the 5,000lb of death. The four-storey building was completely demolished and 260 marines were killed. At the same time another suicide trucker hit the French Paratroop company HQ in Beirut and fifty-eight soldiers died in the gigantic blast.

On 21 September 1984 a Moslem suicide truck bomber crashed into the compound of the US Embassy in Beirut, while the British ambassador was visiting his American counterpart. US Marines opened fire with M16 automatic rifles at the speeding truck as it headed for the underground car park, but missed the driver. An instant later, a corporal of the Royal Military Police, one of five armed bodyguards protecting the British ambassador, triggered an accurate burst from his German Heckler & Koch MP5A3 submachine gun and riddled the driver's cab.

The driver slumped over the wheel and the truck, packed with 500lb of TNT, veered sharply away from the entrance of the underground car park and exploded, wrecking the British Embassy vehicles which helped shield the main building from the worst of the explosion. Eight people died and forty-seven were injured in the blast. Had the truck penetrated the underground car park the death toll would have been enormous. The crackshot army cop had prevented a massacre.

British Army wall chart of the Sterling L2A3 that replaced the Sten.

British soldier armed with 9mm Sterling SMG, now outmoded by the SA80 automatic assault weapon. (Photograph by John Norris)

9 mm Sub Machine Gun L2A3
Technical Data

WEIGHT Gun and full Magazine	3·6 kg
Magazine Capacity	34 rds
Sighting Range	100 and 200 m
Cyclic Rate of Fire	540 rpm approx

position. The delayed roller locked bolt system also allow the weapon to be held more easily when firing bursts.

The SAS used the HK MP5A3 (with retractable butt stock) when, in May 1980, they successfully stormed the Iranian Embassy in London to free hostages held at gunpoint by terrorists. Again the right training and the right weapon delivered excellent results: five terrorists were shot dead and the sixth was captured. In the USA, Senator Henry Jackson extolled the SAS exploit as 'the best in professionalism in dealing with terrorism for a long, long time. It was clever, it was smart and it was tough.' The *New York Times* also praised the SAS action:

> The audacity and precision of the Special Air Service's commandos reaffirm the intrepid British image of a Winston Churchill, a Francis Chichester, or even a James Bond. 'Who Dares Wins' is the commandos' motto: they dared, and they saved real lives in fourteen electric minutes.

UZI and Beretta SMGs

Two other notable 9mm SMGs which have seen wide service with military and security forces are the Israeli UZI and the Italian Beretta PM12. The former, designed by Colonel Uziel Gal of the Israeli Army in the late 1940s and introduced in 1954, won a fine reputation in Israel's lightning six-day war of 1967 and in many paratroop and commando raids into hostile territory.

The UZI designed by Colonel Uziel Gal of the Israeli Army and manufactured by Israel Military Industries.

In the Falklands War of 1982 British troops distinguished themselves in a series of fierce firefights against a prepared, dug-in and well-armed enemy. The UK land forces, which included the Parachute Regiment, Royal Marines, two battalions of Guards, the Gurkha Rifles, and the SAS, defeated the Argentine army of occupation not by the employment of superior, more sophisticated infantry weapons (as the Argentines claimed), but by sheer guts and professional fighting ability.

Both sides were armed with 7.62mm self-loading rifles based on the Belgian-designed FN FAL pattern. However, the Argentine version was capable of automatic fire fed by a 20-round box magazine, whereas the British type (L1A1) had only single-shot capability. The British Army was slow to adopt an automatic rifle, regarding it as wasteful of ammunition, and trained its infantry in single-shot excellence and vigorous use of the bayonet.

The British standard issue submachine gun was the 9mm Sterling with a 32-round magazine; the Argentines had a similar SMG in the PA3-DM with a 25-round box magazine. There was also parity in general purpose machine guns and both forces used the Browning 9mm automatic pistol. It was not superior weapons that defeated the Argentines, but superior skill at arms and leadership.

The 2nd Battalion (2 Para) and 3rd Battalion (3 Para) The Parachute Regiment won further glory for the 'Red Devils' in the Falklands and added another two Victoria Crosses to their roll of honour. The first British airborne unit was formed late in 1940. The red beret and the motto UTRINQUE PARATUS – Ready for Anything – were adopted, and the Germans dubbed them 'Red Devils' because of their ferocity in combat.

In the battle for Darwin and Goose Green on 28 May 1982, 2 Para was commanded by Lieutenant-Colonel Herbert ('H') Jones. The advance was held up by an Argentine trench system on a ridge. The British sustained heavy casualties and the attack was in danger of faltering. 'H' Jones saw clearly that unless desperate and daring measures were taken immediately the attack would fail. It was time

RED DEVILS IN ACTION

for personal leadership and action.

The colonel grabbed a Sterling SMG and, supported by a small party, charged the key enemy position with total disregard for his own safety. His uphill assault exposed him to cross-fire from several trenches. Near the crest he fell, but picked himself up and continued his lone charge, firing from the hip. Almost on his objective, Colonel Jones fell, mortally wounded.

Inspired by their commander's bold action, the Paras swept forward, yelling and shooting. Corporal Abols wiped out a machine gun post with a direct hit from his 66mm rocket launcher and won himself the Distinguished Conduct Medal. The Argentines, their will to fight undermined by the colonel's heroic endeavour, now quickly surrendered to the determined Paras. Colonel Jones was posthumously awarded the Victoria Cross.

In storming the fortified Mount Longdon on the night of 11/12 June, 3 Para suffered considerable losses in killed and wounded. The long, craggy height was held by the stubborn Argentine 7th Regiment reinforced by specialist elements and snipers. The Argentines had prepared their defences system for over two months and were equipped with sophisticated night viewing aids, sniper sights, heavy Browning machine guns, 120mm mortars and 105mm guns.

British artillery and naval gunfire supported the night assault of 3 Commando Brigade. Throughout the hours of darkness the Paras pressed forward relentlessly, engaging each bunker in turn, and needing all their resources of weaponry, tactics, and sheer guts to overcome a determined enemy dug into the rocks in battalion strength along the mountain top. By first light (0600 hours) the Paras had taken Mount Longdon with rifle, grenade and bayonet.

Sergeant Ian McKay, 4 Platoon, B Company of 3 Para, single-handed cleared an enemy bunker with grenades but was killed in his moment of triumph. He was awarded the Victoria Cross. The Parachute Regiment received a total of sixty honours and awards in the Falklands Campaign. 'Red Devils' indeed!

Red Devils of the Parachute Regiment armed with the 7.2mm L1A1 Self-Loading Rifle (SLR). They took part in the Falklands War of 1982.

OPERATION 'MAGIC FIRE'

In October 1977, four armed terrorists hijacked a Lufthansa Boeing 737 from Majorca and held passengers and crew hostage, demanding the release from West Germany of eleven imprisoned terrorists. After flying to Cyprus, then Dubai and Aden – where the plane's gallant captain was shot dead by the terrorist leader, who called himself 'Captain Mahmud' – the aircraft landed at Mogadishu in Somalia. While the West German government played for time with the hijackers, a thirty-strong team of GSG-9 counter-terrorist commandos flew to Mogadishu to deal with the problem. The operation was code-named 'Magic Fire', and the commandos wer armed with excellent SMGs produced by the West German firm of Heckler & Koch, the HK MP5 submachine gun and the HK self-loading pistol. GSG-9 men are trained to fire the MP5 from all positions and in crowded conditions. With the German squad went two members of the SAS, Major Alastair Morrison and Sergeant Barry Davies. Their presence on the mission was cleared by top level agreement in Britain and West Germany. The SAS men took with them a crate of stun grenades. Invented by the SAS especially for anti-terrorist operations, this grenade contains magnesium and explodes with a loud bang and brilliant light, sufficient to blind and stun temporarily an unprepared enemy for six vital seconds. It may frighten the hostages but will do them little or no harm.

Just before 2am on 18 October operation 'Magic Fire' was set in motion. The GSG-9 commander instructed the Somalis to light a diversionary fire on the edge of the airfield to attract the attention of the terrorists in the grounded aircraft. A few minutes later the assault team, faces blackened, armed with HK MP5s, pistols and stun grenades, crept up on the aircraft and positioned themselves. The SAS men were first to strike. They blew open the emergency doors situated over the wings and tossed in stun grenades.

With the cabin filled with blinding light and deafening noise, the GSG-9 burst into the aircraft through the forward and rear doors, shouting 'heads down!' in German. The passengers ducked for safety and bullets flashed and cracked over the seats. The shooting was all over in five minutes. The accurate fire of the commandos shot dead three of the terrorists, including the ruthless 'Captain Mahmud', and wounded the fourth. Four passengers and one GSG-9 man were slightly injured. It was a spectacular feat of arms.

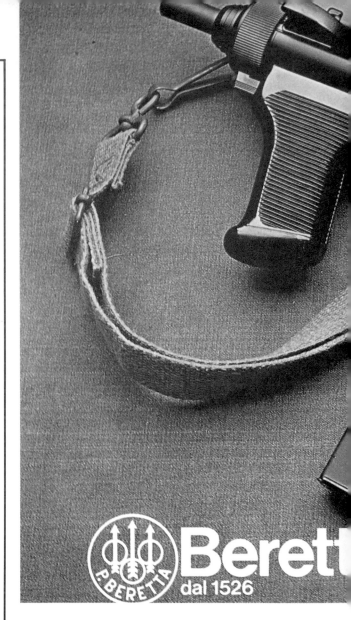

The UZI's compact size derives from the so-called 'wrap-around' bolt system and the magazine housed in the pistol grip. The later Mini-UZI reproduces the original design in a smaller compass: overall length of the Mini-UZI with metal stock folded is 360mm (14.17in). It has a cyclic rate of 1,200 rounds per minute and is fed by magazines holding from twenty to thirty-two rounds.

The Beretta PM12 (Pistola Mitragliatrice) went into production in 1958 and in 1961 was adopted by the Italian Police Force and by the Carabinieri. In 1977, the model was improved by having the safety and the fire-selector switches combined in a single lever, and as such became the PM12S. The selector allows for easy choice of three positions – safety, single shot, full automatic – without any need to remove the hand from the grip. The automatic safety, which locks the trigger and the bolt in its closed position, safeguards from accidental firing if the gun is dropped and precludes firing if the grip is not firmly held.

PM 12 S
cal. 9 mm. Parabellum

Advertisement for the Beretta PM12S.

FIGHTING WITH A SUBMACHINE GUN

The Sten and the Thompson could be carried either slung over the shoulder, or upside down at the trail, like the rifle, or in front of the body with the sling round the neck. When the enemy is likely to be met, the 'ready' position can quickly be adopted from any of these positions. Bring the weapon close in to the right side with the butt under the arm, and the barrel pointing to the front, grasping the pistol grip. Cock the gun, grasp the foregrip with the left hand, and close the right forefinger round the trigger . . .

There were three methods of firing: from the shoulder, using the sights; from the shoulder, roughly aligning the barrel on the enemy but without using the sights; and from the waist, firing by sense of direction. The position used will depend on the circumstances. Sights should always be used if time permits, and fire from the waist only when speed is of great importance.

The position and method of firing from the shoulder, using the sights, is the same as for firing a

A Dyak tracker of the Malayan Security Forces, carrying an Australian Owen SMG during an anti-terrorist operation in the 1950s. Note the unusual top-mounted vertical magazine.

rifle, except that the enemy should be faced squarely, as when firing a pistol. When firing from the shoulder on an enemy who has suddenly appeared, swing body from the waist, at the same time bringing the SMG into the shoulder and quickly point the muzzle at the enemy, roughly aligning the barrel. The position of the feet is immaterial, provided that balance can be maintained. While firing, observe the strike of shots if possible, and correct the alignment of the barrel as necessary.

Fire from the waist is not accurate, and should be reserved for when taken by surprise by the enemy. Speed is of the essence. Swing the body from the waist as before, and fire straight from the 'ready' position entirely by sense of direction, making every effort to observe results and correct the aim. In an emergency, fire can be applied from the waist on the move, but if it is possible to halt momentarily, greater accuracy will be achieved.

Paratrooper of the French Foreign Legion in the 1960s armed with the MAT49.

American soldier of World War Two at Jungle Training Center, Hawaii, firing a Thompson M1A1.

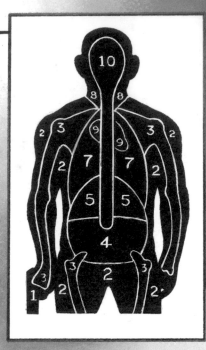

10
A FISTFUL
OF FIREPOWER

Just before Lieutenant Winston S. Churchill, 4th Hussars, left England to join General Kitchener's Anglo-Egyptian army in the campaign to reconquer the Sudan, he purchased a new type of pistol at the London establishment of Westlcy Richards and Company. It was a German Mauser semi-automatic, or self-loading pistol, Model 1896 in 7.63mm (.30in) calibre with a ten-round box magazine. And during the battle of Omdurman, on 2 September 1898, the gun saved Churchill's life.

Kitchener's force confronted a formidable Dervish army controlled by the Khalifa Abdullahi, the successor of the Madhi whose followers had killed General Gordon and occupied Khartoum in 1885. Now the British were back to settle the outstanding account. At Omdurman, the Dervish soldiers attacked in strength but were repulsed by heavy artillery, rifle and Maxim gun fire. Kitchener ordered the 21st

Lancers to leave the defensive position and reconnoitre the southern flank. Churchill, on attachment to the 21st, commanded a troop.

In pursuit of a small party of the enemy, the lancers were lured into a trap: a dry riverbed in which some two thousand warriors lay concealed. Suddenly, the 21st Lancers, 320 strong, were launched into a full-blooded charge. Churchill, recovering from an injured shoulder, decided to use his Mauser instead of his sword. He drew the pistol from its wooden holster and, at the gallop, brought it to the full cock. He wrote about the charge in *My Early Life*:

The collision was now very near. I saw immediately before me, not ten yards away, the two blue men [Dervishes] who lay in my path . . . I rode at the interval between them. They both fired. I passed through the smoke conscious that I was unhurt . . .

With lancers falling all about him, Churchill kept his seat and barged through the savage mêlée and scrambled his horse up the other side of the watercourse.

> Once again I was on the hard, crisp desert, my horse at the trot . . . Straight before me a man threw himself on the ground . . . simultaneously I saw the gleam of his curved sword as he drew it for a ham-stringing cut. I had room and time enough to turn my pony out of his reach, and leaning over on the offside I fired two shots into him at about three yards. As I straightened myself in the saddle, I saw before me another figure with uplifted sword. I raised my pistol and fired. So close were we that the pistol itself actually struck him. Man and sword disappeared below and behind me. On my left, ten yards away, was an Arab horseman in bright-coloured tunic and steel helmet, with chain-mail hangings. I fired at him. He turned aside. I pulled my horse into a walk and looked around again.

Churchill saw the Dervish mass re-forming. He saw two riflemen kneel and take aim at him. He wrote:

> For the first time the danger and the peril came home to me. I turned and galloped to rejoin my troop – having fired exactly ten shots and emptied my pistol – but without a hair of my horse or a stitch of my clothing being touched.

He was lucky indeed to emerge from the fierce engagement unscathed. Hardly a survivor of the regiment, man or horse, came through without some injury, slight or serious.

The Mauser Model 1896 was the first successful automatic pistol to see wide military service. It needs to be said at this point that the term 'automatic' when

Lieutenant Winston Churchill (Simon Ward) uses his German Mauser self-loading pistol during the Battle of Omdurman in 1898. (A Scene from the film *Young Winston*, 1972, courtesy of Columbia Pictures Industries Inc.)

applied to self-loading firearms is really a misnomer. An 'automatic' pistol should more properly be called semi-automatic to distinguish it from a true automatic or machine gun capable of continuous fire. A semi-automatic or self-loading weapon will, after each shot triggered, eject the empty case, load a fresh cartridge from the magazine into the chamber, and leave the action cocked ready to fire again when the trigger is pulled. However, a number of modern automatic rifles can fire either single shots, three-round bursts, or continuous fire like a machine gun.

French Army heavy mortar team armed with the 5.56mm FAMAS automatic assault rifle. (Photograph by John Norris)

SEMI-AUTOMATIC PISTOLS

The Luger

The 1890s saw the appearance of various pioneer semi-automatic pistols, of which the Borchardt and the Mauser are the most noteworthy. Hugo Borchardt, a German-American, patented his self-loading weapon in 1893. The Borchardt recoil system incorporated a folding toggle joint to lock the breech-block. It was a practical pistol (over three thousand Borchardts were produced in Germany) but cumbersome, fragile, and in need of much improvement. George Luger, an engineer with the Deutsche Waffen und Munitionsfabriken (DWM) factory, where the last of the Borchardts were turned out, greatly modified the awkward and ugly proportions of the Borchardt and patented a number of improvements.

Luger's weapon was named the Parabellum Pistole and it became a classic in design and a famed military sidearm. The term 'Parabellum' was inspired by the Latin motto SI VIS PACEM PARA BELLUM – 'if you desire peace prepare for war'. Lugers made between 1900 and 1942 were chambered for the 7.65mm (.301in) and 9mm (.354in) Parabellum cartridges. The Swiss were the first to adopt the Parabellum – generally

The Luger type still produced today by Erma-Werke of West Germany.

called the 'Luger' – as a service pistol in 1900. Improved models came in 1906 and 1908, the latter model being adopted by the German Army and designated 'Pistole 1908', abbreviated to 'P08'. Made in various barrel lengths, the P08 and the Model 1914 served the German forces throughout both world wars.

There is a story concerning a Luger and Tom Horn, the professional gunman of the Old West. In 1903, Horn was in jail at Cheyenne, Wyoming, waiting to be hanged for murder. He jumped his guard, taking the latter's new Luger, and ran through the town pursued and shot at by citizens and lawmen. Horn levelled the loaded pistol several times as if to shoot back, but did not. He was recaptured and returned to jail. Horn was used to the simple double-action mechanism of his Colt Model 1878 revolver; he did not know how to work the Luger system. Tom Horn was duly hanged on 20 November 1903.

The Luger Parabellum was produced in some thirty different versions by arms manufacturers of many nations. Production in Germany ceased in 1943 when increasing numbers of the Walther P38 (adopted by the German Army in 1938) began to replace it as the standard service weapon. The Luger, elegant and finely-made, accurate and well-balanced, had its faults: operating parts were uncovered, making it prone to jamming when exposed to grit, dust and dirt. It was also expensive to manufacture and ill suited to mass production. The Walther P38 was cheaper and easier to make and its action was almost completely enclosed, thereby ensuring reliability in adverse conditions.

The Walther

The P38 remains one of the finest 9mm Parabellum calibre pistols ever made. It is a double-action weapon. Unlike most semi-automatics of its time, in which it was necessary to pull back the slide and release it, thus chambering a cartridge and leaving the hammer cocked for firing, pulling the P38 trigger both cocked and fired the weapon. Over one million

German soldier armed with Luger pistol, a stick grenade, and carrying ammunition for the MG34 machine gun. The man behind carries a Mauser Kar 98k rifle.

were made during the war. Although production of the P38 ceased in 1945, it restarted in 1957 for issue as the P1 standard pistol to the newly organised West German Bundeswehr. It is still in production today at the Walther factory.

Carl Walther established his gunshop in 1886 and proceeded to make a reputation for fine sporting rifles. His son Fritz designed the first Walther semi-automatic pistol in 1908. The outstanding Model PP (Politzei Pistole) was introduced in 1929, originally intended for police use. A shorter, lighter version was produced in 1931 and designated PPK. Some sources say the 'K' means 'Kriminal' because it was originally designed as a concealed gun for policemen and detectives. Others maintain that the 'K' signifies 'Kurz' (short).

Operated by simple blowback action and fed by an eight-round magazine, the PP and PPK have seen wide service with the German and other European police, and the German Army and the French and Turkish forces. It is claimed that Adolf Hitler committed suicide with a 7.65mm Walther. The PPK was a favourite of the fictional James Bond and the PP/PPK pistols in 7.65mm and 9mm Parabellum are still produced today by Carl Walther Waffenfabrik GmbH at Ulm, as well as new model semi-automatics and match pistols and target rifles.

Even the best of pistols can malfunction at critical times. In March 1974 an armed man attempted to kidnap Princess Anne from her car in a London street. Her personal bodyguard, Inspector James Beaton, fired his 9mm Walther PPK at the man and missed; when he triggered a second shot the pistol apparently jammed. Beaton was shot three times before the gunman was overpowered. Fortunately, the gallant inspector recovered from his multiple wounds and was awarded the George Cross for his bravery under fire. A policeman and three civilians also received gallantry medals for their part in the incident.

The Browning

The jamming of the Walther influenced London's Metropolitan Police to replace all other handguns

SHOTGUN SHARPSHOOTER

Throughout the 1950s the British Special Air Service (SAS) served in Malaya against the Communist guerrillas, cunning adversaries well-versed in jungle warfare and concealment. To help them hunt the enemy, the SAS recruited Iban Dyak trackers from Borneo. Learning from these native trackers, a number of SAS men became expert in following a human trail, no matter how faint. Perhaps the most notable of the British trackers was Sergeant Bob Turnbull. He befriended an Iban, Private Anak Kanyan, learned the language so that he could converse fluently with both Ibans and Malayans, and became a better tracker than his Iban teacher.

Turnbull developed the ability to snap-shoot extremely fast and straight, an important talent in jungle fighting. His favourite weapon was the Browning automatic shotgun that could fire up to five shots in quick succession, widely used by the SAS in the Malayan campaign. Turnbull could work his shotgun so fast that three shots sounded like one. Turnbull's love for jungle-combat and lethality with a shotgun became legendary in Malaya.

One Turnbull exploit involved trailing four guerrillas for over a week. When he came upon their jungle hut it was well guarded. Experience told him to wait for the impending rainstorm, then take the enemy by surprise. Adverse weather means nothing to a determined SAS soldier. Waiting for the correct time, then winning, is all that matters. When the torrential rain lashed down the sentries entered the hut for cover. Turnbull, soaked to the skin, seized his chance. Crashing into action, he shot all four terrorists.

It was Sergeant-Major Turnbull who ended the notorious career of Ah Tuck, a guerrilla leader noted for his skill with a Sten submachine gun, which he always carried, ready cocked for instant action. When finally these two hunters confronted each other at twenty yards, Turnbull worked his repeater shotgun with such rapidity that Ah Tuck died with his Sten in his hand, unfired. In 1956, Sergeant-Major Turnbull was awarded the Military Medal for his outstanding service in Malaya.

THE GREEN BERETS

Special Forces soldiers of the US Army are, to quote from a recruiting pamphlet, 'A unique combination of Ranger and Paratrooper . . . Physically fit and mentally mature, they have confidence in themselves and faith in their comrades. Specialists in communications, covert operations and intelligence, demolitions and weapons. Each man is cross-trained to take another's place in case of emergency. A special breed of man – that's why they wear the green beret.'

The US Armed Forces have a number of Special Forces (SP) of which the Green Berets are the most celebrated. They can trace their unit lineage back to the First Special Service Force of World War Two. Formed in July 1942 at Fort William Henry Harrison, Montana, the unit was a joint American-Canadian outfit raised and commanded by Colonel Robert T. Frederick. Such was the martial ferocity and tenacity of this elite unit that the Germans named it the 'Devil's Brigade'.

During the 1950s and 1960s the Western nations raised special military forces to fight the spread of armed Communism in their colonies and former colonies. The British reactivated the Special Air Service (SAS) in 1952 for jungle combat in Malaya and elsewhere. The French raised parachute units for service in Africa and Indo-China (Vietnam).

The US Army activated its SP programme in 1952 with the formation of 10th Special Forces Group at Fort Bragg, North Carolina. Fort Bragg is still the home base and training centre of Special Forces. In September 1961, President John F. Kennedy officially authorised the wearing of the green beret.

Originally raised as specialists in guerrilla warfare, the airborne-qualified Green Berets were employed in the early stages of the Vietnam War in a variety of roles: deep reconnaissance into enemy territory, aggressive strike missions, and the raising and training of South Vietnamese civilians into irregular defence groups to combat Viet Cong insurgents from the North. Green Berets in small teams came to control some eighty fortified camps and sixty thousand irregular soldiers.

Many of these camps were attacked by the Viet Cong in force. In July 1964 Captain Roger Donlon of 7th Special Forces Group won the first Medal of Honor (the US Army's highest combat award) since the Korean War of 1950–3. Donlon and his A Team of Green Berets at Camp Nam Dong waged a desperate five-hour

The American Soldier, 1965, Vietnam.
(From the painting by H. Charles McBarron, courtesy of US Army)

firefight against heavy assault from Viet Cong.

Armed with mortars, grenades, Colt automatic pistols, and the Armalite AR15 automatic rifle (an early version of the M16 purchased for evaluation in Vietnam), the small group of Americans and native irregulars held out by sheer will and firepower. Despite suffering multiple wounds, Donlon continued to move around the camp rallying and inspiring his men with outstanding leadership and courage.

Donlon's team (Detachment A-726), including himself, numbered twelve: two were medical corpsmen, Sergeants Gregg and Terrin, and another was Warrant Officer Kevin Conway of the Australian Special Air Service. Conway was killed in the fight, as were Sergeants Gabriel Alamo and John Houston. Terrin left his own cover in an attempt to aid the mortally wounded Houston, but had only gone a few feet when his AR15 was shot out of his hand.

Terrin, momentarily dazed, stood silhouetted against the light of exploding mortar bombs, his shattered left arm and hand streaming blood. Donlon shouted at him to take cover and Terrin jumped into a gun pit and continued fighting with one arm, firing an Armalite from the hip. With his left arm useless, the redoubtable Terrin pulled the pins from grenades with his teeth.

The Green Berets who held Nam Dong received a total of thirty-three US and Vietnamese decorations. Captain Donlon was awarded the Medal of Honor by President Lyndon Johnson and Sergeants Alamo and Houston received posthumous awards of the Distinguished Service Cross.

US Special Forces have operated in many countries. In 1960 a team was sent into the newly independent African state of the Congo (a former Belgian colony) where rival native groups were fighting for power. Caught in the savage violence were many European and American civilians. Lieutenant Sully Fontaine of 10th Special Forces Group and his team were sent to the Congo to gather together and evacuate as many white refugees as possible. Fontaine, a Belgian by birth, had lived in the Congo and knew the country.

Flying in a light aircraft, the Green Berets searched the wilderness for isolated groups of refugees. On one occasion when Fontaine landed near a village he found himself surrounded by screaming, ferocious rebel soldiers out for blood. Fontaine faced the leader and asked for safe passage for himself and the refugees.

US Special Forces soldier on jungle patrol armed with M16 automatic rifle.

'My orders are clear,' snarled the rebel. 'All whites must be killed.' Fontaine pulled the pin from a grenade and handed the pin to the man. 'Then understand this. If you kill me, you die also.' And for two incredible hours the rebel leader and Fontaine stood facing each other, the pressure of the grenade's lever against Fontaine's hand becoming almost unbearable. Rebels and refugees stared in silent fascination at the deadly confrontation. Which man would weaken first?

Fontaine had said his prayers when the situation was resolved by another Green Beret who came charging and yelling out of the bush, firing his submachine gun into the air. With the rebel leader's attention distracted, Fontaine tossed the grenade into the armed mob and made good his escape with the refugees. The Congo rescue operation resulted in the team evacuating 239 refugees without a single casualty. A mission in the true spirit of the Green Beret motto: DE OPPRESSO LIBER (Freedom from Oppression).

The Green Beret Memorial statue at Special Warfare Center, Fort Bragg, North Carolina.

with Smith & Wesson revolvers. However, in July 1977 the Browning 9mm (.354in) semi-automatic was issued for use with the special D11 marksmen team. The veteran Browning HP35, designed by the American John Moses Browning, was introduced in 1935 and has seen wide and distinguished service throughout the world. Browning self-loading pistols have a history stretching back to 1900.

John M. Browning (1855–1926), a brilliant and influential gun designer, was born into a Mormon family of gunsmiths in Ogden, Utah. He designed rifles and shotguns for Winchester and Remington, and several types of machine guns and an automatic rifle. It was Browning who designed the original Colt Model of 1900 semi-automatic pistol that, in modified form, became the long-serving US Government issue Colt 1911A1.

In 1897 Browning joined forces with the Belgian firearms company Fabrique Nationale (FN) and various Browning FN automatic pistols were produced over the years, culminating in the Model 1935, known as the Hi-Power (HP) or Grande Puissance (GP). Browning was granted a patent for his new pistol in February 1927, three months after his death. Although similar in design and function to the .45in calibre Colt Model 1911, the Browning HP35 represented the designer's ultimate refinement of the locked-breech system, operating on the principle of the short recoil of the barrel.

Firing a 9mm Parabellum cartridge contained in a thirteen-round magazine housed in the butt, the HP35 was used extensively throughout World War

Two by the Allied forces – and the Germans. With the Nazi occupation of Belgium, the FN plant produced some two hundred thousand Brownings for the German Army. The Canadian firm of John Inglis, Toronto, took on the production of the HP35 for Canadian and British forces. The pistol was popular with commando and special service units. Inglis manufactured 151,800 Brownings in several marks during the war.

In 1957, the HP35 was adopted as the official sidearm of the British Army and entered NATO service with the Belgian, Canadian, Danish, Dutch and UK forces. The Browning made the front page of a British newspaper on 10 July 1987. Under the headline THE EQUALISER, a picture of the pistol introduced the story of a London police marksman who, as a member of a special team that had ambushed a gang of armed payroll robbers, shot dead two of the gang and wounded the third. The bandits, who had been called upon to surrender, refused to comply and aimed their weapons – two pump-action shotguns and a Smith & Wesson Magnum revolver – at the police. But the crackshot officer was quicker and resolved the highly charged situation.

The Colt 1911

The .45in (11.43mm) Colt Model of 1911, the US Government issue based on John Browning's original design, is an outstanding self-loading pistol with a long and reliable history. At the turn of the century the US Army's standard handgun was the .38in (9.65mm) Colt double-action revolver, adopted in 1892. The Spanish-American War involved the USA in fighting colonial-style campaigns in the Philippines. The southern Philippine Islands were peopled by Muslim Filipinos called Moros (Moors) by the Spaniards. The warlike Moros were recklessly brave in battle and charged in a berserk manner inspired by religious fanaticism and, possibly, a drug-induced superstrength.

The Moros' favourite weapon was a razor-sharp cleaver, generally called a bolo. The Spanish could not tame the Moros, and these fierce and frightening warriors gave the US Army a very bad time. The Moros, it is often claimed, caused the US military to change from the .38in Colt revolver to the .45in Colt semi-automatic, because the .38in bullet was not heavy enough to stop a charging Moro. There are many accounts of officers firing all six revolver rounds into an onrushing Moro and failing to stop him. The army required a bigger calibre to deliver a blunt blow that could drop a man.

After stringent tests and field trials over five years with various semi-automatic models, the US Army

The Browning pistol made front page news in Britain on 10 July 1987. (Photograph courtesy of The Sun)

Sergeant Alvin York, sharpshooting American hero of World War One, wearing the US Congressional Medal of Honor and the French Croix de Guerre.

Tennessean drew his Colt pistol and dropped the advancing Germans one by one. He then resumed firing at the machine gunners with his rifle. As the Maxim fire slackened, York called on the Germans to surrender. The German major in command thought he was facing many more Americans than the resolute York and his seven buddies. The major and about fifty men surrendered.

With his pistol to the major's head, York marched the prisoners towards the American lines; as they did so more and more Germans surrendered and joined the captive throng. By the time they reached battalion headquarters York had collected 132 prisoners. He was promoted sergeant and awarded the Medal of Honor, plus many other Allied decorations. To his credit, Sergeant York never cashed in on the numerous commercial offers that were made to him as a national hero; he took no pride in having killed so many of the enemy. He had simply done his duty as he saw it.

The Colt 1911 was modified and in 1926 was redesignated M1911A1. Millions of these hard-hitting, reliable pistols have been made in the USA, and elsewhere under licence. They served the US Armed Forces well, until the 1980s.

The US Army Beretta

In 1985 the US Government made the controversial decision to adopt a new pistol – a foreign one: the Italian Beretta 92SB-F in 9mm Parabellum (NATO) calibre. The government tests and trials embraced models from the American companies Colt and Smith & Wesson, Fabrique Nationale of Belgium, Heckler & Koch and Carl Walther of West Germany, Star of Spain, and SIG of Switzerland. The American contenders were plagued with breakages and malfunctions. SIG and Beretta emerged as the final competitors after completion of testing in September 1984.

The five-year US contract, valued at 75 million dollars, called for 52,930 pistols of Italian manufacture to be produced in the first year, followed by 65,750 units the second year with US assembly and testing of parts made in Italy. The final three years will see full production at Beretta USA Corporation at Accokeek, Maryland, to manufacture all parts, components and assembly from raw materials purchased in the USA. The Beretta 92SB-F (double-action with fifteen-shot magazine) has evolved from the original, designed in 1976. An earlier model 92SB has been in wide service with military and law enforcement agencies including the Connecticut, Wyoming and North Carolina State Police, and the Texas Rangers.

accepted the Colt Model 1911, which had, in an endurance test, fired six thousand rounds without a single malfunction. US officers and non-commissioned officers were issued with the Colt 1911 when America entered World War One in 1917.

Corporal (later Sergeant) Alvin C. York was armed with the Colt pistol, and the US Enfield Model 1917 rifle, during the remarkable action in which he won the Congressional Medal of Honor. On the morning of 8 October 1918 advancing US forces were held up by intense machine gun fire from a wooded slope on the edge of the Argonne Forest, near Châtel-Chéhéry. A patrol sent out to silence the Maxims ran into heavy fire and lost half its strength. Corporal York found himself in command of seven men surrounded by the enemy. York, isolated somewhat from his buddies, started to pick off the German machine gunners with his rifle. A country boy from Tennessee, York grew up a crackshot hunter and target shooter, and every time a German showed his head, or part of it, York sent a bullet straight to the mark.

Suddenly, an enemy officer led six soldiers in a bayonet charge against York's position. Having exhausted his rifle ammunition, the cool-headed

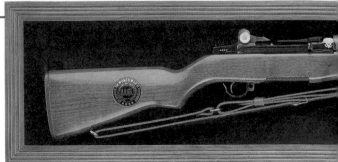

The US Army M1 Garand, a special commemorative limited edition issued in 1985 by The American Historical Foundation of Richmond, Virginia.

The Italian 9mm Beretta 92SB-F with fifteen-shot magazine, chosen by the US Government in 1985 to replace the venerable Colt M1911-A1 as the standard pistol of the armed forces, designated the M9.

The Battle of Bagsak Mountain in the Philippines, June 1913, between US troops and Moro tribesmen. The officer on the left is using the government issued Colt Model 1911 semi-automatic pistol. (From the painting by H. Charles McBarron, courtesy of US Army)

The Soviet AK47 Kalashnikov automatic rifle has been widely used by Warsaw Pact armies, the Chinese, African guerrillas and many others. It is simple, robust and reliable.

US troops armed with M1 rifles and carbines land at Leyte, the Philippines, in October 1944. (From the painting by H. Charles McBarron, courtesy of US Army)

Type 56S, the Chinese version of the Russian classic AK47 Kalashnikov automatic assault rifle.

AUTOMATIC RIFLES

The first self-loading rifle to be adopted as a standard weapon, by the US Army in 1936, was the American Garand M1. Thus the US was the only nation to enter World War Two with infantry equipped with a semi-automatic rifle. Designed by John Garand, the M1 is gas-operated: after firing, some gas is tapped off through a small vent near the muzzle and its pressure operates a piston, which ejects the empty case and reloads the weapon from an eight-round magazine. It was an excellent rifle for its time, but it was heavy at 4.313kg (9.5lb) and a popular Carbine Model M1 at 2.36kg (5.2lb) was introduced in World War Two.

Foot-slogging GIs also had the additional firepower of the .30in (7.62mm) Browning Automatic Rifle Model 1918, a gas-operated, air-cooled weapon that, heavy though it was, could be fired from the shoulder or the hip. Fed by a box magazine holding twenty rounds it fired single shots or bursts. The BAR could also be fitted with a small bipod to serve as a squad light machine gun, with a cyclic rate of 500–600 rounds per minute.

The Kalashnikov AK47

Late in the war the Germans introduced the Sturmgewehr 44, first of a new style weapon, the 'assault rifle,' a hybrid of the orthodox rifle and submachine gun. The most successful and widely used assault rifle to date is that designed by the Russian Mikhail T. Kalashnikov and introduced in 1947 – the Avtomat Kalashnikova, the AK47. An improved and lighter version, the AKM, came in 1959. Kalashnikov, born

The M1 Garand in action with US soldiers during the Korean War of 1950–3.

in 1920, served as a tank commander in World War Two. Severely wounded in the battle of Bryansk, he was invalided out and turned his talents to gun designing. His guiding principles in creating the AK47, simplicity, reliability, and effectiveness, were brilliantly achieved. Simple in design, production and operation, durable in adverse conditions and inured to rough usage, it can deliver single shots or full automatic fire at the practical rate of 100 rounds per minute, fed by thirty 7.62mm (.300in) cartridges housed in a distinctive banana-shaped magazine.

An unsophisticated weapon (compared with the American M16 assault rifle), the AK47 has proved the ideal arm for untrained insurgents and guerrilla forces. It has been manufactured by most countries of the Communist bloc with national variations to the basic design. An estimated thirty-five million Kalashnikovs have been produced, world-wide, making it the most prolific firearm of all time. A modern variant, the AK74 is chambered for a smaller cartridge, in line with the general military trend. The Israeli Galil assault rifle was directly developed from the AK47, with a modified gas system and the addition of a folding stock and bipod, the latter for use in a light machine gun role.

The M16

The American M16 was a radical departure from conventional design and construction, with a straight line configuration and chiefly made of fibreglass and aluminium alloy, giving maximum strength and minimum weight. This ubiquitous automatic started its long career in 1954 as an original concept by Armalite Inc, then a subsidiary of Fairchild Aircraft, and the M16 is still referred to by the generic term Armalite. Then known as the Armalite AR15, the rifle was purchased for evaluation in the early 1960s by the US Air Force and the US Army, the latter

The M16 in the capable hands of members of a US Navy SEAL (Sea-Air-Land) Team, a commando-type outfit.

Soviet paratrooper armed with the AKM, an improved, lighter variant of the AK47.

US Special Forces patrol carrying M16 rifles.

The M16 cast in bronze for posterity: detail of the Vietnam War Memorial in Washington DC.

US Marines boarding helicopter transport on aircraft carrier to be lifted into action.

The British SA80 automatic rifle designed at Enfield\and officially adopted by the British Army in 1985.

testing it thoroughly in the Vietnam war. By 1969, the US forces had adopted the M16 as the standard rifle. Over six million have been produced for armed forces throughout the world.

The M16, modified and manufactured by Colt Industries, progressed through the M16A1 to the M16A2 now in current service with all US forces. The M16A2 is a lightweight 3.4kg (7.9lb) gas-operated shoulder weapon capable of semi-automatic, and either full automatic or three-round burst control fire, using 5.56mm (NATO) ammunition; it has a thirty-round magazine capacity and a cyclic rate of 600–940 rounds per minute.

The M16 system's straight line construction with the barrel, bolt, recoil buffer unit and stock assembled in line, disperses recoil straight back to the shoulder, while keeping barrel climb to a minimum. The bolt locks directly into the barrel, eliminating the need for a heavy steel receiver, while a unique gas-operating system eliminates the conventional operating rod normally associated with gas-operated weapons. The M16A2 is also made in smaller, more compact carbine and commando versions for use with paratroops and special forces.

The British L85A1 Rifle

In October 1985 at Enfield, Royal Ordnance made the official handover to the British Army of the new weapons system, designed and developed at Enfield, that would eventually replace the veteran L1A1 Self Loading Rifle (SLR) and the 9mm submachine gun as standard issue. Known as the SA80 (Small Arms 80), the new 5.56mm (NATO) calibre automatic rifle was given the army designation L85A1. This individual weapon (IW), a combination rifle and submachine gun, is shorter and lighter than the outmoded SLR.

In basic design the gas-operated SA80 and its companion the Light Support Weapon (LSW) are the same, but the LSW has a longer barrel, a bipod, and a

rear pistol grip to give it increased range and accuracy when fired in the light machine gun role. The buttless, straight line configuration enables both weapons to be fired from the shoulder, hip, sitting or prone positions. Recoil is much reduced, thus improving target accuracy in comparison with other heavier calibre small arms.

Both weapons are easy to field strip, and no special tools are required. The trigger mechanism is a self-contained assembly attached to the main weapon body by two captive pins. The pressed steel main body houses the breech mechanism assembly and guide rods. The barrel is fixed to the body by screwing into the barrel extension which is welded into the body pressing. The non-metallic handguards are fixed to the body/barrel but have a removable cover for access to the gas system.

Capable of automatic or single-shot firing, ammunition is fed from a thirty-round magazine which is interchangeable with the American M16 5.56mm magazine. Its standard flash eliminator enables muzzle-launched grenades to be fired. Both the IW and LSW can be fitted with the robust high performance SUSAT (Sight Unit, Small Arms, Trilux) optical sight which enables the weapon to be used more effectively and enhances operational performance under poor light conditions. The SUSAT requires no maintenance. A night sight can also be fitted. This compact rifle is expected to serve British soldiers well into the next century.

Corporal David O'Connor, Royal Marines, being chaired off Century Range, Bisley, having won the 1987 Queen's Medal for shooting. He holds aloft the SA80 that he used to win a number of events of the meeting.

AMBUSH IN VIETNAM

During the night of 18 June 1967 a ten-man squad of the US 196th Light Infantry Brigade set an ambush near the hamlet of Phuoc An in Quang Ngai Province, South Vietnam, in the hope of waylaying Viet Cong (VC) insurgents.

Squad leader Sergeant Lloyd E. Jones, a graduate of the 25th Infantry Division Ambush Academy and a thoroughly professional soldier, was no stranger to ambushes. But for four of the patrol this would be their first firefight.

Jones determined that the rice paddy terrain

Air Support. US Phantom jets aid hard-pressed ground troops in Vietnam. (Painting by George Akimoto, 1966, for the US Air Force Art Collection)

US Marine on jungle patrol. (Courtesy of US Army)

in which he would be operating offered no significant tactical advantages to his squad and explained to them that it was liable to be 'a pretty hairy affair'. Simply stated, their mission was to ambush and then capture or kill any enemy moving in the area.

Company standing operating procedure specified the equipment to be carried. Each man would carry four hand grenades. Seven were to be armed with M16 automatic rifles; two with M15 rifles that had been issued for test purposes, and two with M79 grenade launchers and Colt pistols.

The riflemen were issued with ten to twenty magazines each in varying mixes of tracer and ball ammunition. The grenadiers, in addition to three extra pistol magazines, would pack between them sixty-four high-explosive rounds, eleven canister rounds, and three illumination flares.

Jones decided not to include an M60 machine gun in his arsenal since three riflemen with ample ammunition, in his opinion, would provide the same firepower without the strain on mobility that a 23lb (10.4kg) machine gun would impose. He also decided to take along five claymore mines, three smoke grenades, two flashlights and a strobe light, the latter for signalling a medical evacuation helicopter if required.

Each man would carry water (no food would be taken), a first-aid packet, and a small towel for suppressing coughs and sneezes. Soft caps, not helmets, would be worn. As patrol leader, Jones would have the only map of the area and the only compass, and a two-star cluster signalling device. Using a sketch, Jones explained to each of his ten men where his position would be and what was expected of him. He gave the patrol's radio frequency and call sign and instructed his men to be ready to move out at 1900 hours.

It was 1930 hours and still daylight when, having cleaned and test-fired their weapons, the patrol left the base camp in squad formation: fire teams abreast, Team A on the left and Team B on the right, 40m apart. On reaching the ambush site, a trail junction, Jones deployed his men into four groups, two groups of two men and two of three men.

On the eastern flank he stationed one three-man group as a security force and ordered the emplacement of two claymore mines along the trail. He placed another three-man security group on the western flank, also covered by claymores. The other two groups were centred on the junction. By 2010 hours the ambush party was ready, occupying a position some

40m from flank to flank with roughly 6–8m between each group. Jones made radio contact with Company HQ.

Some forty-five minutes later Private James H. Lee, using a Starlight telescope night detection device, spotted six armed Viet Cong moving in single file towards the ambush. The waiting Americans tensed for action. On entering the killing zone the VC halted. The lead, or point man, who was only a few feet from Sergeant Jones's position, signalled to his comrades.

Fearing he had been detected, Jones detonated a claymore and the point man disappeared in the explosion. The rest of the squad opened fire with M16s and grenade launchers. The claymore explosion triggered enemy fire from the rise of ground some 25m from the trail junction, and a VC submachine gun was sweeping the trail with sporadic bursts.

Private Robinson, on the right flank security position, took on the enemy SMG with bursts from his M16. In the adjacent two-man team, Private Grooms also fired at the SMG and threw grenades towards the muzzle flash. Suddenly, all VC firing stopped, and Jones ordered one man from each team to go forward and 'police up' the area: a quick search revealed only the dead body of the point man and his Chicom 9mm SMG.

Mission accomplished, a satisfied Sergeant Jones radioed HQ that he was returning. Before leaving he detonated the remaining claymores. Two of the squad had sustained wounds but not serious enough to warrant a call for helicopter evacuation. The patrol reached base camp just before midnight. The return trip took much longer because Jones, the experienced veteran, took a different route to avoid being ambushed himself.

Shortly after daylight next morning the patrol returned to the ambush site, where a second body was discovered together with an American Thompson SMG with three full magazines. And from bloody clothing and other evidence at the scene, Jones concluded that his men had probably killed or wounded two more of the enemy during the firefight in the dark.

Adapted from *Ambush at Phuoc An* by John A. Cash in *Seven Firefights in Vietnam* published by the Office of the Chief of Military History, United States Army, Washington, DC.

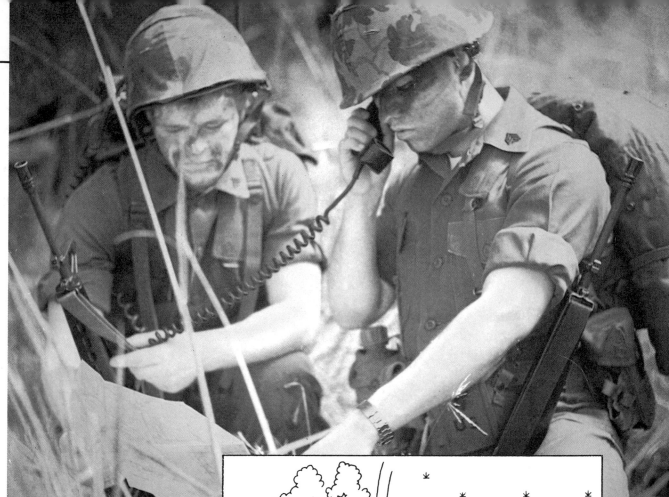

Patrol leader of US Marine Corps using the all-important radio communications link. (Courtesy of US Marine Corps)

Plan of the ambush positions set up by Sergeant Jones at Phuoc An, South Vietnam, on 18 January 1967. (Courtesy of US Army)

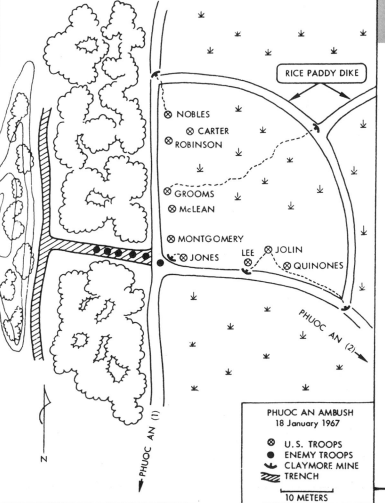

RICE PADDY DIKE

⊗ NOBLES
⊗ CARTER
⊗ ROBINSON

⊗ GROOMS
⊗ McLEAN

⊗ MONTGOMERY
⊗ JONES
LEE ⊗   ⊗ JOLIN
⊗ QUINONES

PHUOC AN (2)

PHUOC AN (1)

N

PHUOC AN AMBUSH
18 January 1967

⊗ U.S. TROOPS
● ENEMY TROOPS
⚓ CLAYMORE MINE
▨ TRENCH

10 METERS

A sniper's target. Radio operator silhouetted against sundown.

SNIPERS

April 1965. Near Da Nang, the US airfield in the north of South Vietnam, the Viet Cong sniper raised his rifle and locked his telescopic sight on a target: the head of a young US Marine, Private J. D. Goff. It was the luckiest day of Private Goff's life.

The instant before the sniper squeezed the trigger, Goff raised his rifle to the firing position. The Viet Cong bullet entered the barrel of Goff's M14. A fantastic freak shot. The barrel split open, sending fragments of metal into his face, but he was not seriously hurt.

Snipers are a useful element on any battlefield. A camouflaged marksman in a concealed forward position can take out enemy leaders, or a radio communications man; he can pick-off machine gunners and pin down units of advancing infantry. A sniper in the dark using a night scope is a fearsome, phantom hunter who can create a climate of *angst* among the enemy.

Modern technology in firearms and telescope sights, especially night vision devices, has greatly increased the capability of trained

A British Army sniper in his hide armed with 7.62mm L96A1 sniping rifle. (Photograph by John Norris)

snipers. The Starlight Scope, for example, in service with the US Army, is a battery-powered image intensification device that works with a minimum amount of moonlight, starlight or skyglow. Such a device gives the sniper a clear view of his target at night.

Sniping has a long history. In the American War of Independence the splendid 'Kentucky' rifle, in the hands of backwoods marksmen, took heavy toll of the British redcoats. The British responded by hiring German sharpshooters. The American Civil War saw the introduction of telescopic sights, used notably by Berdan's Sharpshooters of the Union Army. Sniping reached optimum heights in World War Two when standard issue military rifles were adapted and developed for that special purpose. Both the British and Argentines employed snipers in the Falklands War of 1982.

German snipers of World War One were greatly respected by their Allied enemies, who quickly learned to keep their heads down in the years of trench warfare. The main German sniping rifle of that war was the Mauser Model 1898. Normally the bolt lever of the Mauser stuck out straight, but the sniping version had a special turned-down bolt and a large-capacity magazine holding twenty rounds. Among the

excellent 'scopes available to the German sniper was a Zeiss-made sight for shooting in the dim light of early morning or at dusk.

In World War Two the US Army established sniper schools to teach the fundamentals of the role; in the special outfits of the Army Ranger and Marine Raider units, snipers were given specialised training and proved highly effective in both the Pacific and Europe. The famed US Marine Corps snipers used the bolt-action Model 1903 A1 Springfield with the specially ordered Unertle 8-power telescope, a 'scope almost as long as the rifle barrel. Late in the war a battery-operated electronic device called the Sniper Scope was developed for use with the M1 Garand semi-automatic rifle.

The British Army opened a school for snipers in 1940 at the celebrated Bisley range, to instruct selected recruits not only in marksmanship but also in the art of camouflage, concealment, fieldcraft, and stalking the enemy. A sniper is required to have great patience and endurance, for his task demands that he remain in a concealed position, often cramped and cold, for long hours with little sustenance, waiting for the right target and the right moment to strike.

The Japanese sniper of World War Two demonstrated plenty of patience and endurance and proved adept at camouflage and concealment, especially in trees. The Japanese jungle marksman was equipped with climbing spikes for his boots and would strap himself to a tree. He used a special smokeless sniper cartridge which gave off no flash. The Japanese sniper was a stubborn fighter, staying at his post until discovered and killed. Few were taken alive.

Modern sniping rifles are specially designed, rather than being standard issue weapons adapted for the role. In some models the traditional bolt-action single-shot rifle has given way to semi-automatic design. The Soviet Army was first in the field with a semi-automatic sniping rifle, the Dragunov, based on the action of the AK47 Kalashnikov and fitted with a long barrel for accuracy. The Israeli Galil Sniper is also a gas-actuated weapon using the same mechanism as the semi-automatic Galil assault rifle.

British sniper in full flower showing the special design of the new L96A1 sniping rifle.
(Photograph by John Norris)

British soldier with the SA80 automatic rifle of the 1980s.

THE FUTURE INFANTRYMAN

What will the infantryman of the future look like? What kind of weapons will he carry? What tactics will he employ? Scicon, a leading computer company, has researched and presented a clear vision of the infantry soldier of the twenty-first century. The main changes are likely to result from advances in computer technology. The company has predicted that the size of micro-computers by the year 2000AD will make it possible to provide the foot soldier with extremely advanced integrated systems that are not only easily portable but immensely powerful. These systems would include secure and rapid communications, target laser-designation for strike fire, a thermal imager, moving-terrain mapping displays, and a helmet-mounted 'eyes-up' display of battlefield information.

According to Scicon, tomorrow's Individual Weapon (IW) will be a two-barrel design. It will provide local protection in firefights against dismounted infantry and lightly armoured vehicles. The upper barrel will fire high-explosive, anti-personnel, smoke or illumination rounds. The lower, for close-in self-defence, will fire a small-calibre caseless round. Maximum effective range will be 400m. The IW will be aimed through helmet-mounted systems and fired by trigger. If the computer systems fail, there will be back-up manual controls and conventional sights.

Electronic technology will make tomorrow's battlefield more dangerous than any in history. It will change the nature of fieldcraft. To the eyeball of Human Mark I, the modern battlefield appears to be deserted. Soldiers use cover at all times. Look at the elbows and knees of his combat suit: they are worn thin. He has to be careful: to the kind of thermal imagers now entering service, soldiers behind even the densest foliage are clearly visible targets. But, regardless of the technology, a land battle will still be built up from small groups of men defeating other small groups of men. The infantryman will still have to win the firefight using, primarily, his own skill and judgement.

Scicon's Infantryman 2000. *An imaginative vision of the computerised specialist soldier of the twenty-first century.* (Courtesy of Scicon Ltd)

BIBLIOGRAPHY

ATKINSON, JOHN *Duelling Pistols* Cassell & Co, 1965

BALDRICK, ROBERT *The Duel* Chapman & Hall, 1965
BLACKMORE, HOWARD *British Military Firearms* Herbert Jenkins, 1961
BODDINGTON, CRAIG *America: the Men and their Guns that Made her Great* Peterson Publishing Co, 1981
BOUTELL, CHARLES *Arms and Armour* Reeves & Turner, 1874

CHAPEL, CHARLES *Guns of the West* Coward-McCann, 1961

DEMMIN, AUGUSTE *Arms and Armour* George Bell & Sons, 1901
DILLIN, JOHN *The Kentucky Rifle* Washington, 1924
DIXON, OLIVE *Life of Billy Dixon* P. L. Turner & Co, 1927

EDWARDS, WILLIAM *Story of Colt's Revolver* Stackpole Books, 1953
EDWARDS, WILLIAM *Civil War Guns* Stackpole Books, 1962

GEORGE, JOHN *English Pistols and Revolvers* Small Arms Technical Publishing Co, 1938
GLUCKMAN, ARCADI *US Muskets, Rifles and Carbines* Otto Ulbrich Co, 1948

HAMMER, KENNETH *The Springfield Carbine on the Western Frontier* The Old Army Press, 1970
HANGER, GEORGE *To All Sportsmen, Farmers and Gamekeepers* J. J. Stockdale, 1814
HANSON, CHARLES *The Plains Rifle* Stackpole Books, 1960
HATCH, ALDEN *Remington Arms* Rhinehart & Co, 1956
HELD, ROBERT *The Age of Firearms* Harper, 1957
HICKS, JAMES *Notes on US Ordnance 1776–1941* Modern Books & Crafts, Inc, 1971
HUDDLESTON, JOSEPH *Colonial Riflemen in the American Revolution* George Shumway, 1978

KAUFFMAN, HENRY *The Pennsylvania-Kentucky Rifle* Stackpole, 1960
KOURY, MICHAEL *Arms for Texas* The Old Army Press, 1973

MELEGARI, VEZIO *Great Regiments* Weidenfeld & Nicolson, 1969

NEWARK, TIM *Medieval Warlords* Blandford Press, 1987

PARSONS, JOHN *Smith & Wesson Revolvers* William Morrow, 1957
PETERSON, HAROLD *Book of the Gun* Golden Press Inc, 1962
POLLARD, MAJOR *A History of Firearms* Geoffrey Bles, 1926

ROOSEVELT, THEODORE *The Rough Riders* Charles Scribner, 1899
ROOSEVELT, THEODORE *Ranch Life and the Hunting Trail* Century, 1901
ROSA, JOSEPH *Guns of the American West* Arms & Armour Press, 1985
RUSSELL, DON *Lives and Legends of Buffalo Bill* Norman, 1960
RYWELL, MARTIN *Samuel Colt* Pioneer Press, 1955

SABINE, LORENZO *Notes on Duels and Duelling* Crosby, Nichols, 1855
SERVEN, JAMES *Colt Firearms from 1836* Santa Ana, 1954
SHIELDS, JOSEPH *From Flintlock to M1* Coward-McCann, 1954
SMITH, WALTER *Small Arms of the World* Military Service Publishing Co, 1956
SMITH, WINSTON *The Sharps Rifle* William Morrow, 1943
STEINWEDEL, LOUIS *The Gun Collector's Fact Book* Arco Pub, 1975
STEVENS, CAPTAIN *Berdan's US Sharpshooters* Price-McGill, 1892

WILLIAMSON, HAROLD *Winchester, the Gun that Won the West* Combat Forces Press, 1952

British jungle
patrol, armed with
the SA80
automatic rifle.

INDEX

US Airborne soldier collecting his personal equipment after landing by parachute. Note the black M16A2 rifle.